The Poetical Works in Progress

of

Carole Elizabeth Sawo, BSc. (Hons), MA.

Nóra
Best Wishes
Carole Sawo

Hebe Publishing Company

Pandora's Panacea

First publication in Great Britain

ISBN NO: 978-0-9556470-0-0

The author of this book is not a medically trained physician or traditionally trained psychotherapist. All ideas, opinions and thoughts regarding process, procedure and remedial action are given in order to assist overall healing, and are not intended to replace the medical or legal opinions of trained professionals or courses of action advised. Consult your physician or therapist regarding any condition that may require diagnostic, medical or psychological attention.

Published by Hebe Publishing Company

…. for my Soul

With unending love and gratitude for
my absent friends 'in high places'

Hidden

What wonder lies behind the veil

What phantasies within

What secrets may you try avail

What first unconscious sin

What memory have you forgot

What beauty shall you hide

What dream the gatekeeper begot

Beyond the mortal side

Contents

From Mourning into Morning

Prefatory

To See a World in a Grain of Sand
And a Heaven in a Wild Flower
Hold Infinity in the palm of your hand
And Eternity in an hour

William Blake *(1757-1827 - Auguries of Innocence)*

Early one morning, I awoke to the sound of falling rubble coming from within the chimney-stack. In the twilight of dawn I put on my nightgown and crept downstairs to explore. Upon entering the lounge I heard the sound of fluttering wings coming from the fire-hearth, wherein I found a very dishevelled blackbird gripping desperately onto the soot-covered grate; its wide eyes gleaming in the dimness of a heavily curtained room. The blackbird seemed as startled to see me as I was to see it, and I wondered how best I might pick it up without frightening it further. For a moment I considered a cloth and was just about to open the curtains, when from apparently nowhere I remembered a piece of useful information - birds always fly towards the light! As quickly and as silently as I could, I by-passed the curtains and instead opened the front door. In an instant the blackbird flew out into the new morning sun, but in nothing like an instant did I realise the profundity of that event until some time later. Let alone appreciate the intuitive wisdom of knowing when to open, or when to leave some curtains closed.

Of all the hours, months and years that I had spent studying, it was the incident with the blackbird in which I had perhaps learnt the most. In one moment it had flown carefree in the early morning sky, when in the next it had fallen into the blackest hole from within which it must have thought there was no escape. Being unable to spread its wings in order to return to the former blue skies of freedom, the blackbird had crash-landed inelegantly, and most probably painfully, onto the charred embers of a thankfully cold fire. After a moment of apprehension at the new sensations that must have bombarded its senses, it sprang by natural instinct and flew straight out of the open door, toward the light of a new day. The symbolism within such a seemingly small event over time lit up like a hologram. In pure synchronicity, the blackbird revealed something so utterly amazing and completely obvious that I nearly missed it. It had shown me the archetypal pattern of a definitive flight-path. A pattern that traced the circular blueprint of everything; of man, of a spirit, of reincarnation and re-birth - of life! It was that which I had found written into every teaching, that necessarily involved a descent into darkness, fire, light and resurrection; all of which preceded a spiritual ascension and conscious evolution. It was not only the clumsy capers of a blackbird that I had witnessed that morning, but the structured flight of the mythical phoenix, forever rising from the flames of purification. Before me too, illuminated the fundamental process of chemical transmutation. Though more, much more than that, the blackbird had shown me the spherical journey of a dearly beloved soul, Heaven's own alchemical vessel capable of extraordinary transformation - it had shown me the flight-path of us.

As the blackbird fell down the chimney, it may have grasped as we often do in life, for a handle, lever or brick on which to hold. But chimneys, like life, are designed circular for a very good reason. Had the blackbird found a temporary ledge upon which to perch, somewhere between the light above from which it could not return, and the darkness below that seemed its only terrifying option, then it may have, as we often do, gotten stuck in the tunnel of its own fears. Getting stuck in the chimney is to us the equivalent (and precursor) of a potential illness; at first in the mind and then in the body. In response to a life event we easily become disorientated, frightened, lost, unstable. In panic we try to go back to the familiarity of yesterday but cannot and neither are we able to move on to tomorrow. We feel paralysed, helpless, trapped, vulnerable and so we seek ledges upon which to stabilise, people on whom to frantically cling. Most of which are only plasters of temporary solution that we desperately hope will never come off, though we inevitably find that they do. In pain we seek a hero, an idol in the external world to fill the void in the internal one. When in truth the only hero that can rescue or save us, is the one that lives forever within. We have lost touch with the saviour on the inside, and that is the real problem we all face today. For many, 'within' is the absolute last place they would ever think, or rather, would ever want to look. Even if given a map of their internal world and a way out of the material maze by celestial satellite navigation. Directions to 'go within' can seem irritatingly futile when everything on the outside appears to be falling apart. But a solution is always found in the problem and if the problem is in the inside, then there too is the solution.

Tumbling straight down the chimney without any option, the bird would have been undoubtedly afraid. My lounge with all its material stimulants could never have vibrated at the frequency of freedom, no matter how much I had sought to cleanse it. Like us the blackbird fell awkwardly into darkness, though fortunately it had landed into a cold fire. But not all descents are into cold fires, as we and the phoenix can testify, but then again, neither are they supposed to be. Since it is often in the fires of our apparent private hell, that not only our eyes but our hearts and minds might be opened. Where 'no-ledge' for the ego yields knowledge for the Self. And where our souls may be ever more purified, even if the timing between furnace and flight seems unbearably painful and unfairly extended. It is there in the cooling embers and light of a new day, that we may find not just the cinders of carboniferous charcoal, but the essence of the carbon-arc coalesce.

For many hours I pondered the fall of the blackbird, that in my mind perfectly epitomised the first fall of man and beloved child of God, Adam; of whom it is written did partake of the forbidden fruits of Eve and was forever cast out of the Garden of Eden; in a momentous expulsion portrayed beautifully by Milton in *'Paradise Lost' (1667).* Others have written that Adam never left Eden, but that his 'fall' was into an unconscious sleep from which he (and we as descendants) has yet to wake. To me, Adam's fall symbolises not only the unconscious sleep of an innocent child, but the conscious pursuit of a dreaming man who forever seeks to regain the innocence that he *perceives* has been lost. But there is nothing like ignorance to keep a man guilty, bound and blind. When in reality innocence can never truly be lost only ever hidden, or more specifically, misperceived. An exile from Eden is nothing more than a descent into the shadows of sleepy illusion, into a dream of a loss and a departure from the light of awakened Truth. The flickering eyes of the blackbird reminded me of that which I had written years before in summation of an essay, when my flickering *internal* eye had perceived, 'that I finally realised I had gone to University to learn so much that one day I would simply remember – not just how to *act* like a child, but how to *be* one'. It was the plight of Peter Pan who had forgotten how to fly, how to be a child, who feared that leaving the nursery meant that he would have to leave behind his youthful innocence. It was a recurring archetypal theme about which I had happily written as I left behind children playing in a classroom, 'that whilst I recognised I too had to leave the nursery, there was just no way I was ever going to grow up'. Because to me innocence and maturity were two separate things, though they co-existed as two threads on the same needle. We seemed to grow out of mature innocence and in to immature guilt. And whilst I knew life was going to present me with less than the joyful moments to be found in a nursery, to 'grow up' in any conventional sense, was to 'grow out' of my innocence and deny that a part of me was always going to be a child. It was to deny my wondrous imagination, my creativity, self-expression, my spirit and my soul. And to deny all of that, was not only to deny I was alive, it was to deny who 'I' really was.

Life is full of things to be afraid of if we choose to perceive it as such. Children however, unless taught otherwise, do not perceive of a world with fear and trepidation, but with amusement and laughter. They utilise that which the adults have forgotten and through the use of a playful imagination, easily transform a potential travesty into an opportunity for comedy and fun. In play they use few words but communicate with hearts, and they happily accommodate the evolutions within their inner worlds alongside their ever-changing outer ones. Children are not only the innocent followers of adults, but the teachers of innocence within them. In their newness on Earth they still love as purely as Heaven does – unconditionally. They have not yet learned to impose conditions upon love or turn it easily into hate when their attempts to manipulate it fail. They do not perceive of differences, nor use them as excuses to distance and attack, but naturally extend their love into everyone else. Children assess not the face but the heart for beauty and when life presents with a challenge, they use their own natural instincts of humour and trust. Every child is a gift from Heaven, a beam of light that reflects and projects the mind of Divinity - a mind from which Adam, like us, was not only created in the image, but in the imagination of God. We are not born sinners, but born into ignorance and it is up to each and every one of us to educate ourselves out of it. 'Paradise' is found the instant we recall and embrace how amazing we still are, even if surrounded by cave dwellers who try to persuade us otherwise. We are many things, not just one thing. To need to cling to society labels or old identities, is to be afraid of embracing who we really are; it is to stay gripping onto a fire-grate, onto the collective cot bars behind which we remain too afraid to fly whilst we project our feed-on-demands; it is to rage through life with a blame mentality, looking always for unconscious revenge on the one who cut the umbilical. But God, thank God, does not think like we do! Descents into darkness are not the punishments for when innocence is lost, but the consequence of an unconditional love forgotten. As Milton wrote in a *'Paradise Regained' (1671)*, it is a love found once more when man is, "Home to his mother's house private return'd." In this world when conscious pursuit introverts and humbles itself before the alchemical chambers of the matriarchal womb - in Eden, when Adam knows Eve as his Self.

No-one wants to fall down that far in life, but we do. Descents are just part of the process of evolution: of a mind, a heart and a soul. In the fall into my lounge, the blackbird may have learned a very important lesson that day, if only not to perch on chimney tops. Having passed through a cycle of re-birth, perhaps it had emerged better learned, more awake than before and maybe even a little more wise. Were the embers hot, it is possible the blackbird's physical life may have ceased to continue on, though I am absolutely sure that its spiritual life still would have. 'Phoenix moments' are not just for birds, but for anything that experiences life. On Earth is where we do the *work* of transformation, where every external war reveals only a war in the internal world, projected out in an effort to disown it. It is where we negotiate the hidden agendas in our own hearts and minds, where we hopefully strive not for a hostile take-over, but a diplomatic resolution attained more easily when grace has been invited in. In descents we are called to ask fundamental questions about our realities and ourselves – in 'phoenix moments' we may find the answers. Incarnations do not always require that we physically cease, they require that we metaphysically shed our old feathers of yesterday, in order that we may grow stronger wings for tomorrow's flight. They challenge us to let go inherited, out-dated unconscious belief structures, all in order for a conscious evolution and a unified spiritual enlightenment. 'Phoenix moments' force us to bear the pain of the fires of purification, in order for some essence of wisdom to be revealed; a process that can only serve to enhance and fine-tune our flight-paths through this life, and eventually, our ascension through the ethers back home.

I had played an important part in the blackbird's experience that day, as it had played an important part in mine. I could have sought to capture it, being bigger and questionably more bold, both in my pure wish to be closer to nature and also in my ignorant desire to control it. On reflection, I was glad that I had opened the door out of intuition whilst the blackbird flew past out of instinct - we had both lived on to see another day. Later, I discovered that the blackbird was the symbol of the enslaven soul and I wondered if in its surrender it had secured its own release; I was thankful that in an instant I had set it free. Had I conversed with the bird right after, it may have described a plummet into the darkest place, a frightening giant looming in the twilight with tufts of hair and huge feet. When I might have replied, that in truth and fairness at 5am, it was a sooty chimney, a warm nightgown and comfortable slippers - though it might go to show how we often perceive things in the opposite and selectively choose that which we wish to see. Of course in that moment the blackbird had not uttered a word, although in a manner of speaking perhaps it had. As I finished the collation of this book, I smiled in reflective recognition: that it was in truth a morning had broken; when I'm sure that a blackbird had spoken; it had sung of both the first and the last word – and in Eden, I saw play!

And there to Eternity aspire
The selfhood in a flame of fire
Till then the Lamb of God

William Blake *(1757-1827 - Morning)*

Introduction

"I say unto you: one must still have chaos in oneself to be able to give birth to a dancing star. I say unto you: you still have chaos in yourselves".

Friedrich Nietzsche *(1883-1885 – Thus Spoke Zarathustra)*

I had no intention of writing a book, let alone ever publishing one – I guess my soul had other ideas. My love of poetry began as a small child. I loved the way that apparently anything could be conveyed within a poem, in a way that seemed conducive to both the mind and the heart. Some poems made me laugh, some made me feel, some didn't really make sense at all and yet others had the ability to focus my attention and make me think - really think. No matter who or how skilled the poet, all poems seemed to point to at least one fundamental truth in life; though it was not until I was much older that I discovered the true 'poetry of poetry', it was a perfect medium of communication and a wonderful way in which to access not only the inner sanctum of the human heart, but the deepest caves of the human mind. Poetry is a philosophical archaeology, capable of extraordinary excavation. Intrinsic, is a licence that easily by-passes conscious assessment, as an eternity of memories illuminate in the eternal maze of the subconscious mind. Just as in the joke or the dream, poetry takes on board rational reason, condensing and combining it effortlessly with irrational thought. It is secretive and obvious, misleading and meaningful, complex and simple; and yet time over again, within and between the lines are insight, honesty and wisdom. As a language, poetry makes up its own rules, exploiting an innate infinite lexicon within the dormitory of imagination. As an art form, it easily holds its own amongst many other great forums of expression. Poetry possesses an amazing capacity to sooth the troubled mind, console the broken heart, free the bonded spirit – poetry has the power to commune directly with the soul.

Over the past few years I have been privileged to analyse not only poetry, but many other great works of art such as painting, sculpture, children's stories, fairytales, and the most wonderful masterpiece of all that is the human mind – or perhaps more accurately, the 'piece of the Master' that is our mind. The more I explored each individual piece, the more I found buried deep beneath the intricate, unique, yet superficial layers of difference, was a fundamental element common to all, and that element was a language. It was the language of my mother tongue that I adored, it was that of the amazing unconscious. In artwork it was known as *iconography* and in psychoanalysis it presented, or rather re-presented in exquisite *symbolism*. Artwork, like us, began to reveal more than the physical eye could perceive; it shone in text so pure that only the inner eye could read it, and whispered in a tongue so subtle that it was almost inaudible. It was a tongue that beautifully ignored the differing languages to be found in argument at the bottom of Babel's tower, where individual importance sought only to savage the advancement of a collective intellect. I found a language containing no words that told of a world with a deeper meaning than anything else to be found in the material realm. It was the language of Nature, of life, of love - and its only sound was silence.

In silence artwork skilfully mediates between many worlds at any one time. As windows of perceptual opportunity, all pieces deserve more than to be left on dusty shelves or hung pretentiously in empty halls. Great masterpieces have less to do with artistic skill and more to do with creative depth. They invite the perceiver into not only the artist's, but the perceiver's imagination, reflecting all that is within there. Masterpieces ask questions, offer answers, tell stories; they are transitional objects, descriptions of a journey, a collation of transferences from childhood experience - they are pictorial representations of an autobiographical sketch. Like us, the masterpiece is multilayered, revealing different aspects at different angles, dependent always upon the mind of the subjective perceiver. The masterpiece is the mirror that reflects the questions we did not even know to ask; revealing an unconscious reality too blinding for many to fathom, 'that often what they see is not just what they get, but that which they have already given.' Viewed up close the masterpiece is the multifaceted crystal that reflects all that is within us. Viewed from a greater dimension, they appear the living holograms that they are.

Artists, by some descriptions, are those eccentrics who it might seem sometimes fly too far from the conventional linear box; but they are also those marvellous beings with open minds capable of producing timeless works, that not only permit everyone else an escape from the rigours of daily life, but wonderfully point to a reality more ethereal in existence than this. Artwork is the immortal gift for the often thankless mortal, who prefers to perceive of a mad artist in favour of an insightful prophet who has paid dearly the cost of bringing ancient wisdom back to the tribe. In every piece is to be found the 'real life' experience of the artist, together with a snapshot of their mind at the time of its creation. In parchment, canvas and marble are captured not only the projections of an imaginative mind, but a replica of one.

Of all the amazing 'holograms of enchantment' that I have studied, there are a few, mentioned here, that particularly caught and held my attention for different reasons: *'The Scream'*, by Edvard Munch *(1863-1944)*; *'The Moses'* and *'The David'*, by Michelangelo Buonarroti *(1475-1564)*; and my all time favourite, *'The Wonderful Wizard of Oz'*, by L. Frank Baum *(1856-1919)*.

'The Wonderful Wizard of Oz', by L.Frank Baum (1856-1919)

Whilst it is not unusual to find ancient wisdom woven within a children's fairytale or nursery rhyme, such as that found in *'The Land of Far Beyond'* by Enid Blyton *(1942)*, in *'The Wonderful Wizard of Oz'*, I found in addition, a complete description of an extremely important and very real human experience. Like everyone else my age, I had watched the film every Christmas when I was a child, and later my attention was drawn back to the story by a question on an essay paper that simply asked, 'If life were a film, book or drama, which one would it be?' For me the choice was intuitively obvious. What was not so obvious at the time however, was that the story would transpire to be not only a phantasy fairytale rich in exquisite, multi-disciplinary symbolism, but a narrative of a phantasy reality that many people still lived out today. With the landscape of Oz exactly mirroring the topographical landscape of the unconscious, the story was a complete account of the interior of the human mind and the characters, or rather the archetypal structures, that lived in there. Of much more interest however, was that the author, Lyman Frank Baum, had given a brilliant, direct description of a very real, often terrifying human experience - an evolution of consciousness within the human psyche and the ego's reaction to it.

At the time of writing, Baum had to bear many projections of persecution. His work was ridiculed and banned in some countries and his character attacked by wild accusations. Later he had to endure the ultimate insult; the last shout of a dying tribal chief in a vicious attempt to strip a wonderful mind from Divine insight, was to label it mad and 'balmy'; but Baum was not the crazy one. Like so many other creative minds capable of performing psychic acrobatics, Baum was a literary genius. In his 'real life' he grew up in 'Rose Lawn', New York; moving after marriage to 'the windy city', Chicago. His fairytale reveals not only a trip in childhood phantasy, but a highly detailed description of his adult biography; with all the usual archetypal patterns inherent in a collective butterfly script.

~ *the cyclone (up to speed by slowing down)*

Readers are welcomed into the story to join Dorothy the orphan (representative of the inner child), who becomes caught up in a cyclone that carries her to the far-off land of Oz. Dorothy, as the name translates 'a gift from God', is also the name of a saint; the Virgin Martyr and Patron of Floristry who symbolises the *Soul* and *Flower of Life*; with her ever faithful friend Toto (of totem), the *life instinct* and animal nature of the clandestine family spirit eternally by her side. In relation to the human experience, the cyclone describes a mind in a chaotic spin as psychic energy speeds to raise the level of consciousness needed for a spiritual ascension. In

Hinduism, it is the *kundalini*, which translates from Sanskrit, meaning 'coiled like a snake'. In yogic or holistic language, it is the *kundalini rising* of formerly dormant energy in the base of the spine, that suddenly rushes up the spinal column in a spiral motion of DNA unlocking; which often overwhelms the human psyche, creating in its wake a powerful wave of psychic energy that floods the shores (or sures) of consciousness - which is as potentially devastating as that of the Tsunami. The experience can appear as a complete psychic breakdown, though in reality it is a psychic break-up, a fragmentation or 'snow-doming' of the psyche. Anatomically it is the phenomenon of *hyperfrontality*; psychologically speaking, it is experienced as 'unprecedented fogginess', as all that is usual given to conscious awareness is pulled, drawn backwards away from the frontal cortex into the primary brainstem. As everything that has gone before is brought forward in a rush, memories, wounds, heartbreaks, fears, phobias and unconscious beliefs are all washed up into conscious awareness, with many spilling forward into everyday reality, where the drag of the *centripetal force* (the centre of the petal), attracts the bizarre and mysterious into the chaotic. Mid-life becomes turbulent as psychic life is forcefully shoved into reverse. External normality changes in correlation with internal normality; all in order for the purpose of resolution and healing, though in life it can be experienced as a detachment from reality and a trip into spiritual phantasy. In analytical terminology *usurping the ego* is often interpreted as a psychic disorder; in spiritual language as a '*near-death' experience.* As the mind opens psychic ability increases, allowing voices from the spiritual realm to be heard. In sacred text, it is when 'Heaven calls', experienced within the mind as a voice from above and beyond - or more specifically, from behind. As the 'shocked' mind re-orders, it is a time for rest, meditation and prayer; it is a time for silence and the regeneration of a soul. Luckily for Dorothy, whilst she was "awakened by a shock", ECT did not exist in Oz, and she woke naturally to the sight of wonderful sunshine; not so much to the rising of a dawn but the dawning of a rise – and that rise was of her spiritual Self, out of the corporeal realm.

Journeying along *'the yellow brick road'* referring also to Freud's *'royal road to the unconscious' (1900)*, and the colour representative of the solar plexus and life force energy, Dorothy meets with her new friends that signify the virtues one seeks for in life: wisdom, compassion and courage; depicted by the Scarecrow, the Tin Woodman and the Lion. The Scarecrow, who claims to be without a brain and says, "I don't mind my legs and arms and body being stuffed, because I cannot get hurt…But I do not want people to call me a fool, and if my head stays stuffed with straw instead of with brains, as yours is, how am I ever to know anything?" The Tin Woodman, who confesses that when he rusted in loveless solitude, he held up an 'axe to grind' and said, he "had time to think that the greatest loss I had known was the loss of my heart". And the Lion, who explains that he has no courage at all; though later in the story, it is the Lion upon whose back Dorothy 'leaps to the other side of the ditch', in a highly symbolic *leap of faith* where courage is shown to be the necessary component in a mind about to *quantum leap* – out of the confined box and into the unexplored territory of the unconscious, portrayed by every reference to a 'dark forest' (in Oz and Freudian literature).

The *kalidahs* symbolise the parasitical demons that fester within wounds, giving chase to an evolving mind and an ascending spirit. In chopping down *'the crossing bridge'*, the Tin Woodman re-enacts the separation of 'the savage' from the holy oak, into the abyss of illusory misperception. In anatomical language, the bridge represents the *corpus callosum* that links the two hemispheres within the brain; and the leap is the sudden surge of energy that crosses the passageway. Psychologically, the account depicts the moment when the two hemispheres interact at high frequencies; in analytical language, it is the life force that suddenly overwhelms the death instinct, in order to heal the inner dissociations. Spiritually, it is the wielding of love (the axe) that has the power to sever the ties that formally bound the imprisoned spirit to the savages of yesterday.

As the Scarecrow, Lion and Tin Woodman reveal formerly 'hidden' qualities, as with all archetypal structures of archaic origin, there emerges a semblance of light and dark forces at work; reminiscent of *Zoroastrian* duality most obviously personified by the good and bad witches that illustrate not only the bipolar pendulum of dynamic compensation at work in the mind, but also the polarity within the physical brain cell. In mystical language, the witches refer to the battle between powerfully opposing feminine forces: as seen in the dual faces of the Oracle of Delphi (echoes of Jung's *'anima'*) as the good witches of the North and South; positioned vertically on the *axis of ascension* (the spinal column); and by perpendicular contrast, the fearful Medusa, portrayed by the wicked witch of the west that resides in the left hemisphere (in Oz and within the mind); that seeks always to pervert the course of enlightenment by the dispensation of an oblique force, and the distracting influences of western materialism. The Medusa, is a projection from the fragile ego and is a highly powerful double cross, appearing in the dream as a symbol of the 'opposite inverted'. It is the witch in the 'mirror mirror on the wall', that signifies one of the ultimate tests of intuitive faith at high frequencies. The mystical stepping-stones through the psyche are thus: the sequential appearance of the good witch, the bad witch, the bad wizard and the good wizard; with the latter perhaps pointing to Jung's archetypal *'wise old man'* (1959); and the ironically named 'old Father time', being of the Hermetic in both nature and origin.

~ *the deadly poppy fields (the red chakra: into the infra-red)*

Along the journey, Dorothy and companions wander into the most dangerous place of all (in Oz, the mind and human energy system), *The Deadly Poppy Fields*; that portray and demonstrate the powerful sleepy mechanism of seduction at work; to all things addictive: such as opiates, narcotics, alcohol and perhaps one of the most dangerous addictions of all, a psychological disorder. Generally speaking, if there appears a complex of pain then one has already been seduced by a delusion; that relies on a secondary function of anonymity in order to perpetuate. In other words, part of the power of a complex is that it seduces the sufferer into its nucleus, away from the boundary of perception and clarity; its primary objective is to function in denial. Addiction to anything is a never-ending hamster wheel of eternal folly and sufferers have got to get off. To be seduced, one has to have previously taken something in (physically ingested), or have been taken in (psychologically invested). Vulnerability to seduction is due to the inner child's desire to seek satiation of an internal hunger, and its inability to manage the excitable forces of *arousal* in the adult world. In literal terms, an unsatiated spiritual hunger of the soul leads the empty to seek physical satiation through oral or sexual means. Empty children seek satiation through sweet food, and later, affection, fulfilment and primal survival through sexual means - which is a course of action that often leads them into arenas of unprotected danger. The young woman becomes the erotic dancer on the 'phallic pole', who seeks to control and satiate through the predominately male weaknesses of seductive temptation and sexual hunger. The young man seeks to control and satiate through the predominately female weaknesses of seductive attention and blinded flattery. Both genders become vulnerable to the dark forces in life and escape is much more quickly enabled the sooner one recognises they have been entirely tricked. There is an old saying, 'let pain be your guide' and in this instance pain has an up-side, in that if it hurts that much it is probably an indicator of a toxic mechanism of seduction at work; the remedy is to walk away as quickly as possible, or if one has been rendered incapable, to crawl if they have to. In holistic therapy, the red of the poppies points to the red of the base chakra, although I do not believe red to be at the base of the chakra system, but only at the base of the window of human perception. It is that which vibrates 'at low frequencies' and contains many of the most important and difficult lessons in life; lessons that are to do with aggression, sex, erotic phantasy, money and self-esteem are often said to be bound to the red chakra. 'Seeing red' however is not the focus, learning how to manage that frequency of excitation is. Red is also the colour of power and the harnessing of that energy is the aim of the intellect. Abstinence retains the energy to satiate the soul.

~ *the nights of remembrance (the black chakra)*

> *"Does my shadow call me? Of what account is my shadow! Let it run after me! I – shall run away from it."*
>
> Friedrich Nietzsche *(1883-1885 – Thus Spoke Zarathustra)*

Inside the red petals is the black centre indicative of not only the black hole of the external universe, but the black hole of the internal universe; the human mind and the dark matter that lives in there. The Black Chakra sits below base, in the basement of the psyche; at the base of the spinal column. It is the dumping ground of the Universe, the place into which we project all that we do not want to manage, or in fairness, probably know how to manage. The Black Chakra is the 'rubbish pit of our internal and external worlds' – 'pit management' will soon be the challenge of every individual. Just after one has been seduced by the red, they find themselves in the black – literally! Black is an important colour, although virtually every account of the colour spindle will suggest black is not a colour at all, but is the outcome of subtractive colour mixing. Black is reported as that which is reflected to the eye once all other colours have been absorbed; when many wavelengths have been mixed together. Interestingly, it is not only the colour at the centre of the poppies, but the colour at the centre of the colour spindle; where the brightest light is found at the periphery. Black is the colour that contains, rather than reflects the light. It exists below the frequency of infra-red and our inability to perceive of it as a colour, merely reveals the limitations on our ability to perceive. Black is that which vibrates at frequencies beneath the level of perceptual awareness and is therefore reported to not be there. Its illusory aspect is evidenced in the psychological experiments around *the missing fundamental*; in which the fundamental frequency of a complex tone is artificially created and can be detected, although it is apparently not there. The phenomenon draws attention to a conundrum in life: that not only are we to question that which we can see, but also question that which we cannot. To think otherwise might ensure we are caught up in a type of *ostrich syndrome*. In other words, just because something cannot be perceived does not mean that it is not there.

After all, many things potentially toxic perpetuate in relative anonymity, or in analytical language perhaps, 'in an anonymous relative' or perpetual impersonal other. But it is in our dynamic unconscious projections in which we give our faceless inner demons undue power, that makes them appear more real than our selves.

Going into the black in the mind is to enter the *'Noche obscura del Alma'* of St. John of the Cross (*1619*); *'The Dark Night of the Soul'*, that describes the earthly experience of purification of the self before a celestial communion with Christ. It is a frightening metaphysical experience of a walk or flight through the land of dark illusions, and a temporary loss of touch with reality and all things familiar. In part, the experience is made seemingly more terrifying due to the defensive response of the fragile ego, that projects its own fears that its days in office are numbered. Perhaps the greater the resistance of the ego to purification, ensures the greater number of times one has to enter the dark night; though it may equally be the case that some souls are also more determined than others to complete the *unfinished business* this time around. *The dark night* is a pivotal moment in the journey of a soul, where one finds not only the crossroads at which they are given a question and a choice by the *guardian sphinx*, but the cross of Christianity, symbolising the place where two worlds intersect; it is the 'O point' in the psyche (the azimuth), where multiple realities convene according to the co-ordinates of *sacred geometry*; it is there, outside of judicious logic, where all of Riemann's *interesting solutions* equate the primes to zero, according to the *zeta function*, (*The Riemann Hypothesis - 1859*). In apparent darkness is found the greatest opportunity to broaden a mind and strengthen a soul: where resilience, stamina, tolerance, and the ability to stand and withstand under pressure are cultivated. Should we 'walk through the valley of the shadow – of death may we fear no evil' (*Psalm 23*); particularly when 'death' is another illusion; or at most, a reality according only to the physical realm. Emerging from darkness we might realise that it is wisdom that lets us into the tunnel and the dark night - and ultimately, it is wisdom that gets us out!

As every reader of *'The Wonderful Wizard of Oz'* will note, Dorothy, like us, was not alone in her 'dark night'. Whilst in the centre of the poppy fields it is written that, "her eyes closed in spite of herself", she was however accompanied by the Scarecrow and Tin Woodman; who saved Dorothy and Toto (her life), all because they lacked a human sense – they could not 'smell' and therefore did not judge her. Not smelling in everyday terms translates as 'acceptance'. Whilst contemporary literature emphasises the visual and auditory decoding of other people, olfaction to my mind, is one of the most important of all the human senses. We simply 'smell' each other, as animals do, before conscious assessment. It is our way of communicating and answering unconscious questions to do with tribal origin, belief structures and most importantly, likely threats to personal survival. When Dorothy was down and out, her survival (as ours often does), depended entirely on one thing, the capacity of her friends to accept and support her. Being looked upon and accepted by the eyes of love is often the only way we can learn to see and accept ourselves. A look of adoration contains a hidden potential, a loving gaze has literally the power to save a life!

~ *the kingdom of the heart (the green chakra)*

Eventually arriving at the Kingdom of the Wonderful Wizard, known by another name as the majestic ego (*Freud - 1923-1925*), Dorothy and her companions are ordered to wear green glasses by the guardian at the gate (a forerunner of the sovereign ego), in order to ensure that everything looks better than it really is. Green is a highly symbolic colour in that it represents the colour of the heart chakra, associated in mythology with the Greek Goddess Aphrodite, the daughter of Zeus and goddess of love; and the Roman Goddess, Venus. And it is here in the 'kingdom of the heart' where we find the real *holographic* jewels: In astrology, Venus is the name of one of the planets nearest the sun, referred to as the Morning or Evening Star; which is also the name of the lowest chakra (the Silver Chakra, below black), positioned at the ankle (specifically the Achilles heel) - which perhaps hints to the vulnerability of the heart and the need for the 'healing' of it. In physiological terminology, 'venous' relates to the veins that bring blood to the heart. Though perhaps what makes this particular point in the story entirely fascinating, is that green is also said to be the colour of the *Lapis Exilis*, the precious gem and ultimate desire of the fallen angel Lucifer, lost to him when struck by the sword of the Archangel Michael. One theory suggests that the gem was carved into a chalice, the *Holy Grail* from which Jesus was said to have drunk at *The Last Supper* and that which later caught the blood of the dying Christ. It might be theorised that the *Holy Grail* is not a physical object, but a spiritual essence, and as such, it is the *Sacred Heart* that is the 'objet d'art' and constant target of multi-dimensional forces; with the power of Divine love contained therein, the ultimate prize and precious jewel to hold dear.

In healing practice, there is often experienced a turning of the heart chakra, as the stone that formerly sealed the tomb of the heart is finally rolled away by a more powerful, compassionate force. In theological text, it is described by the 'rolling away the stone' from the tomb of the rising Nazarene on the 3rd day. In spiritual literature, it is an ascension of a spirit that either temporarily or permanently leaves the body and the physical domain. Whether in astrological, physical, spiritual or philosophical terminology, it therefore becomes obvious that all life enters and exits through the chambers of the heart; making it a vital choice into whose hands we place ours! A 'Divine Heart' holds the power of all life and its possessor the command of it. It is symbolised by the *Egyptian scarab* that protects the heart of the departed soul, written in *'The Book of The Dead'* as, "thou shalt make a scarab of green stone, which shall be placed in the breast of a man, and it shall perform for him, 'the opening of the mouth" - which is a reference to the opening of the blue throat chakra (above the green), that enables the unblocking of Adam's apple and a return of the cherubical song from the Universal voice. It is the *stone* not only of the crypt, but of the *philosopher* who strives to reach the blessed heartland of Divine comprehension. In contrast, green is also the colour of jealous eyes, envious of the love another has (depicted by Shakespeare's monster in Othello), though primarily, it is that of the *inner eye* of Venus; that sees only surety of accomplishment. Green is the colour of naivety, of the first-born and I suggest, of the last. It is the colour of the living garden, of Paradise, of Nature, of motherhood - and the 'green grass of home'.

Adorning the glasses within Oz, refers to our tendency to be easily misled by others into believing as reality, that which may only appear in phantasy; 'all that glitters is not gold' – and vice versa. But the heart never lies even if the mind often does its utmost to. Love, until a certain level of consciousness has been achieved, appears as the *Janus head*; the double-edged sword that pierces our hearts; capable of ascending us to the greatest heights and leaving us to bleed in the deepest lows. But then love only hurts when it is conditional. Conditional love orders, clings on and manipulates to control; it fears a loss of oxygen, of life, of a heart and soul - it doesn't let go. Unconditional love is the opposite. It is freeing, uncontaminated, accepting, faithful, eternal - it is by description, without condition. Unconditionally, Dorothy follows the wizard's instructions and sets out to kill 'the wicked witch of the west'; the shadow side of the feminine mystical archetype appearing in many fairytales: such as the wicked stepmother in *'Cinderella'*; Cruella DeVil in *'101 Dalmatians';* or the curiously named 'white witch' in *'The Lion, The Witch and the Wardrobe'*; which is perhaps a deliberate distortion of colour trickery utilised by the heavily disguised. Though one should never form an opinion of a witch in terms of whether she is proclaimed black or white, but by careful observation of the purity of her heart and especially, the motivation of her mind. Irrespective, it might be noted that the slayer always precedes the redeemer and in Dorothy's case (in fact in ours also), the redeemer is discovered to be her Self – restored on '*be halfe*' of her Soul. In symbolic language, in casting the bucket of water over the wicked witch who tried to 'de-sole' her, Dorothy *de-spells* the witch, or rather, ex-spells her. As the wicked witch shrinks, Baum writes, "Dorothy looked at her in wonder"; which translates as: fear disappears when innocence perceives of a higher love; the wicked witch is cast out of Dorothy's internal world - forever.

Returning to *'the Emerald City of Oz'*, in her innocence, Dorothy does that which we as humans have enormous difficulty in doing; she meets with and eventually confronts 'he who ruled by fear', *'the Great and Terrible Wizard'* - her ego.

> *"Stop!' he shouted at him with furious laughter, 'stop, you actor! You fabricator! You liar from the heart! I know you well!"*
>
> Friedrich Nietzsche *(1883-1885 – Thus Spoke Zarathustra)*

As the story goes, it was Dorothy's instinctual spirit, Toto, that tipped over the screen; eventually revealing not a powerful wizard, but a little old man. And so the wizard explains that he never 'meant' to be seen in such a way; it was the perceptions of 'the others' (the tribe), that gave him his power - it had all been a perceptual mistake. Power to the wizard translates in psychological terms as a loss of power to the Self and a resultant low self-esteem. As the screen falls revealing the wizard, as clarity re-enters, or rather, is remembered in the mind, the misdirection of psychic energy is also revealed; the wheel invented - inverted. When Dorothy confronted the 'little man behind the screen' she took back her power and he disappeared, as most fragile egos do, in a puff of hot air. Just like the wicked witch, when challenged by truth, honesty and love, the wizard simply evaporated and vanished – by fermentation; into *'thynne'* air.

In metaphorical terms, Dorothy took back control of her mind, got back into the driving seat, which is the moment in which she regained some order within the chaos. For us, a mind out of control is like a fast moving car without a driver; or worse, it is a psychic 'car-jack' and an accident waiting to happen. Recovery begins the moment we recognise we have to learn how to properly 'work and manage our minds': when to fuel them, drive them, clean them, and most importantly, when to rest them – or better still, when to be completely silent. If we are going to work our minds a marathon, or if Heaven sends 'a bolt from the blue', then we have to learn to rest our minds a marathon too. 'Resting' does not equate to procrastination, or television - unless it's well chosen comedy! Important for rest is that all background 'white noise' should be eliminated; except for the heavenly melody of the old world songbirds; which makes the country the best place to head for. The screen concealing the wizard is also a reference to the *Veil of Maya*, the shroud that conceals the truth from the world of illusions. In the mind, the tipping of the screen is a relinquishing of inherited misperceptions. In Freudian language, it is when the *preconscious barrier* has been 'busted'! In analytical terms, it is the experience of becoming 'conscious of our unconscious' and all of the dynamic structures that live in there. And I would just say one thing more about wizards (and for that matter, emperors with new clothes): it is in the fragility that the problem lies, not in the strength - omnipotence is but a fragile illusion, impotence a means to amend!

~ *the golden cap (the crown chakra)*

And so it was that Dorothy overcame every difficulty and eventually went to see the good witch Glinda, whom she gave the *'golden cap'* to that Dorothy had found in the wicked witch's cupboard; a gesture that symbolises the opening of the crown chakra and in philosophical terms, an important grasp of the elemental gold of alchemy. It is that which is found 'over the rainbow' of the human energy spectrum. The colour gold denotes the soul of man and the masculine pole of the Universe: the 'sol' (colloid) or salt of the Earth (for healing), with which Dorothy performs the will of the philosopher who seeks to transform base metal into gold. Dorothy's escapades can therefore be traced symbolically as a spiritual journey through the human energy system: Dorothy alchemised the red chakra (overcame temptation); proceeded through the black chakra (detox and purification); transformed the heart chakra (restored with love) and found the pot of gold at the end of the rainbow (mystical charm). Dorothy, as the true philosopher that she was, succeeded only due to her endeavours being motivated not by a desire to discover a wealth for the pocket, but a wealth for the heart and soul. Good fortune, after all, is not about being 'well minted', but as every alchemist knows - well luted!

~ the silver shoes (the silver chakra)

Perhaps the most misunderstood and important part in the re-telling of the story of Oz however, was that it was in harnessing the solar opposite of gold, silver, the lunar force of the moon, that enabled a unification of all forces. Silver, in contrast to gold, denotes the feminine aspect of the Universe; the mystical Sophia and the Kali Ma. In alchemy it is the *quicksilver*; the elemental mercury and facilitator of change; and in theology, it is seen in images of the silver serpent coiled around the cross symbolising Divine wisdom. In philosophical writing, the silver moon is said to be at least of equal importance to life, due to its regenerative power to heal within sleep. In physiological terms, it has the capacity to cool the hot headed, to stem electrical activity and coagulate blood-flow in the brain. The lunar element is the much-misunderstood 'night owl within the mind', that recognises the wisdom of waking a dreamer from the rising temperatures of REM; and its capacity to *denature* in parallel. In the darkness of night, it is not the mystical moon but the moonlight shadow that attempts to rake the pond and steal the jewels. As gold is the masculine Father of the Universe, so silver is the feminine Mother of the Universe, and it is the marriage of these two opposites that facilitates the hidden pursuit and eventual transcendence of man; depicted by the facing, entwined serpents on the caduceus rod. In Dorothy's case, her plight ended when she thrice clicked together not red shoes as the film depicts, but as Baum originally wrote, "silver shoes"; thereby manifesting the *cold fusion* necessary for the merging of two polar opposites via a common conducive denominator: whereupon all worlds became one. Dorothy's Self became esteemed, authentic, actualised; like Peter Pan, she became real. Though I would also add one last thing about silver shoes: they are never really lost in the desert; they sparkle like mirrors in the sunshine - all in order to save our soles!

Throughout the fairytale, Dorothy is ever motivated by her wish to go home; which for Dorothy was back in Kansas with Uncle Henry and Aunt Em (symbolic of Freud's parental superego). In analytic terminology, 'home' might be said to be when the Self has been released from the imprisonment of the fragile ego; or when the parental superego reconciles and finally stops arguing! In holistic therapy, 'home' is when the energetic system has been unblocked, allowing for the state of wholeness and health to return and regenerate the system. In spiritual language, 'home' is often not thought to be here on Earth, but in Heaven; as it is Heaven where we come from, it is Heaven where we hope to go home to.

Baum's masterpiece was far and away beyond the conscious comprehension of many readers at the time - and perhaps for some, still is. Whilst the characters symbolise not only the archetypes within the unconscious, the allegorical journey through Oz corresponds precisely with the psychological experience of a mind in transition; with the challenges found in the story mirroring the challenges all of us find in life. Of course there is no way of knowing if Baum realised in 1900, that he was also referring to the colours of the chakra wheels found in holistic and energy medicine, or the experience of the *kundalini rising*. Within the story rich in amazing symbolism, can also be found references to mythology, alchemy, philosophy, geometry and religion; whilst *The Wonderful Wizard of Oz'* translates easily in psychoanalytic language as 'the ego within the mind' - It is not just a fairytale but a multi-disciplinary transcript. It is a narrative of a little child battling through life, in addition to being a complete account of the experience of a mind in the midst of adult mid-life changes. What became obvious by the reaction to Baum's work, was that many were uncomfortable to find mirrored in a book, parts of their own mind that they never wanted to explore. Some people were too afraid or just did not want to work that hard. In preference to becoming archaeologists of their own minds, many people preferred instead to 'keep behind the screen' and remain unknown not only to everyone else, but sadly, to themselves. Being known brings with it a fear that one might find something they wish they had not. Something, I wonder, less threatening than stupidity and cowardice, like love; which to some seems to have the power to shatter not only the heart but the mind; though I would suggest (after a long chat with a mythical wizard), that both are supposed to break. We have become fixed broken and we need to be broken again in order to be fixed. Knowing ourselves beyond the image takes enormous courage, considerable mental energy and a huge amount of spiritual endurance. But psychic acrobatics or not, it is surely the way forward, not just for the individual but for the collective. Projections will always get high when the will of 'King Canute' fails to stand against the tides of Universal change. But *will* is given us not to attempt to obstruct evolutions, but to manage them as best we can. Even if many lessons are taught in public and learned in solitude, suffering is something we all experience and we never know, perhaps a soul is ever more purified when purgatory is consciously volunteered.

'The Scream', by Edvard Munch (1863-1944)

Another fascinating piece of exceptional art in my view, is the painting entitled *'The Scream'* by Edvard Munch. Like others, my initial impression of the painting was that it was a depiction of psychological distress: with a face turned toward the perceiver screaming and two figures in the background perhaps resembling wardens from an asylum, it might at first appear to be a work to be quickly moved past. However, a read of the artist's account of the painting written in his diary on 22nd January 1892 *(Heller 1973)*, revealed, as always, much more beneath the surface. The painting, most interestingly, belongs to a collection of Munch's work entitled 'love', that clearly reveals the artist's preoccupying thoughts at the time. The scene depicts a real life experience in which Munch described he was walking along a bridge in Norway with two of his friends, when he "felt a loud, unending scream piercing nature". A scream, I believe, from the 'twin' *Mother Nature*, in an attempt to draw attention through the receptive open mind of the imaginative artist, to a monumental tragedy in the future, when She would sustain superlative abuse on the matriarchal womb, in the destructive attacks that would take place in 1939 in World War II; that historically utilised a *heavy water* procedure in making the German weaponry which uncannily appeared in the swirling river of catastrophe depicted in the painting: in physical terms, it denotes *deuterium oxide.*

In painting himself as the centre-piece in the painting, Munch seems to display an effort to comprehend in his physical artwork, that which he could not understand in his psychic reality: *The Scream* that had occurred within his internal world, and the resultant spin of his mind into chaos. In one view, Munch is perhaps taking off a social mask of illusory conditioning, in another it is possible to see Freud's *psychic triad* described in his *'Topographical Model of the Mind' (1923)*; with the two figures possibly representing the parental superego, storming-off in some critical dispute along the bridge of the *preconscious barrier.* Munch appears as the infantile id, screaming for insatiable attention in a moment of sudden, terrifying detached vulnerability in an unfamiliar world. To the right of the central figure appears the ego in a dark shaded area in the water, symbolising *the shadow* (Jung - *1960b*) that lurks in the murky pool of unconscious emotions, with boats of hope floating in faith on the tide (and mind) of discontent.

As a hologram, *'The Scream'* is also a condensation of transference projections: reflected, refracted from illusions, memories and images from past experience of probably more than this life. Munch had externalised his internal world and captured it in the painting, providing the perceiver with a pictorial account of a moment of phantastical chaos in which logic clashed impossibly with illogic; where the projections from archaic wisdom that may have led to his enlightenment, were lost to the gain of his startled, indignant ego. After painting and re-painting the picture, Munch very sadly retreated into despair and probably had no idea that his painting displayed not his chaotic melancholia, but his incredible *psychic ability* to perceive of events yet untold. He had also successfully depicted something that to this day still baffles the most educated of minds. In a dramatic experience of evolving comprehension, Munch had painted the very moment in which unconscious phantasy knocked on the back door of reality, breaching easily in its wake the conscious barriers within the mind. It was a scene of apparent psychic disorder, but such is the seduction of illusory misperception. To me, it is an incredible painting of a mind that was three parts along a four-part process, when 'the shadow' overwhelmed and won the battle of his psyche.

Even today, most people are still completely unaware of what that process is and how it is experienced, let alone how it is mastered; since it is a process of merging ambiguities that requires a multi-disciplinary approach in order to comprehend, it is an approach that contemporarily proves unpopular within many ivory towers - irrespective of proclamations. Sadly, Munch never knew that he had in fact accomplished the monumental, unfathomable task of painting the human mind, or that in creation of *'The Scream',* he had answered a fundamental, universal question: that man is not just born a creature of the nature of physics, but the physics of celestial nature - and it was Mother Nature who had screamed.

Having studied open minds when they are said to have apparently broken, I have only ever found one thing: a mind in such a highly evolved state of consciousness that many in the collective simply cannot fathom it - and that sadly includes the sufferer also. Whilst I have never met anyone with a mind that I could not understand, I have met many people who do not understand their own mind. I could say many things about apparent insanity, or other psychological disorders, primarily that I never really believed in them as the only reality, or on many occasions, that they really existed at all; until that was, they were made to! To me, insanity seemed a name given to a symptom rather than an explanation for a cause; and on many presentations, that cause needed educating not medicating. Of course I knew something was happening within the mind that made apparent geniuses cross some invisible boundary and fall into the depths of what appeared a much darker place; something seemed to be happening that ensured reasonable, sensible people apparently lost touch with reality; particularly when given more than one life event in a short space of time, or perhaps more devastatingly, the loss of a love. But then I realised, just like the parasitical squatters that move into an empty house, the absence of love attracted the dark matter in every universe; though it was matter that didn't need to matter, or rather, it was a complex delusion and a trick, a really frightening trick of a mind in which its owner seemed to no longer live; and since behaviour follows thought, the consequences were at worst life threatening. Perhaps the biggest tragedy by far, is that of all the 'Self deceptions', the belief that one is losing their mind when they are not, has to be the worst. That which sometimes appears as 'insanity' is often nothing more than a sudden seductive slip un-recovered, that leads to an exiting of a life that could otherwise have led to a happy ending. It is, in another view, a test of mental resilience and spiritual stamina that turns out to be a necessary psychic tsunami of energetic consumption, that affords the best opportunity for greater clarity – if only one can withstand the *velocity*. The vital ingredients for recovery are those that often only children in this material world still find it easy to employ: such as trust, hope, faith, love and humour; trust in a greater power than anything we can come up with as adults; hope for a better outcome than the one presented; faith in an unconditional loving heart; and the belief in all these things that cannot be perceived through the ordinary human senses. When presented with the unpredictable, children often laugh, not *at*, but *with* their selves; they already know that life and all its follies need not always be viewed as a tragedy, but a comedy - and a Divine one at that!

'The Moses' and 'The David', by Michelangelo Buonarroti (1475-1564)

Artist and artwork are not two separate objects, but points along the same creative continuum. Understanding of one often affords understanding of the other, and so it is with a 'holographic' approach that an answer to a problem can often be found in another discipline altogether. During my studies in psychoanalysis, I was taught how to observe not only that which was there, but that which was not; and so it was in artwork that I also looked to see what was not there; what, if anything, might the artist have left out - and why? In *'The Moses'* I found something wonderful, and not just because of the talent of the artist to find 'the angel in the marble', but wonderful because Michelangelo had left something out – he left gaps!

At first glance *'The Moses'* appears a curious figure: with the Hebrew prophet carved with the body of Adonis and the horned head of the God Pan, captured in a moment of apocalyptic revelation - the ambiguity is more than a little obvious. The statue made me wonder, did ambiguity in artwork appear as a consequence of incongruent duplicity within the mind of the artist; and was this the 'chaos' to which Nietzsche referred? At first glance it seemed that I was peering into a void between two opposing poles, though 'the gap' I was minding, appeared to be widening – and it was in my comprehension. I wanted to understand, but I did not. My observation of a gap and the questions that arose, were not answered by my continuing to study the statue however, but of all things, occurred in a synchronistic moment, as all wonderful things do, whilst I was renovating my home – the metaphor for the soul.

A short while later, I had the pleasure of meeting with another great artist; a real live one, a stonemason …hmm! His skill was undeniable, with the pieces he carved in the village workshop equalling those on show in any museum; he was a tradesman, a craftsman, a gifted old countryman who 'breathed' in the stone - literally. The stonemason carved the beautiful stone mantle that now graces my fireplace, though it was as we discussed how best I might fit the new piece of slate for the fire-hearth, that he uttered words that not only answered the questions *'The Moses'* had left behind, but answered what was a dormant question in psychoanalysis – why do some minds break? Referring to the fitting of the slate into the hearth, he said casually, "remember to leave a gap wont you?" My heart alerted me excitedly to pending wisdom. "A gap", I enquired? "Yes", he replied with a smile, "you need to leave a gap - for expansion." As I drove off you might say, given that I had just received a thunderbolt from the ether, that I absolutely beamed! Can you believe that the stonemason also told me the best way to mix cement was to keep it soft and pliable. As I heard it, he was talking about *plasticity*, not only of cement when the fires in the hearth heat up, but *plasticity* in the mind and the brain cell, when the fires of the heart heat up. Global warming in the external world was mirroring global warming in the internal world and temperature was an important factor; since heat was a by-product, a reaction to an action. Heat in the brain cell caused the *myelin sheath* to weaken, having a direct impact on whether the neurotransmitter system was able to function well or not. At the physical level, the reason why some brains could cope when others could not, was because some people's 'oily diets' enabled greater tolerance in the brain cell. Straight forward functioning equates to straight forward thinking and vice versa. People whose minds are in high states of evolution often do not think straight forward – on the contrary, given the surge of electrical activity, they also think sideways, and straight up. I realised that in the case of a psychological disorder, recovery all boiled down (if you'll pardon the gaseous pun), to the agility of not only the brain, but the mind to cope at high frequency communication. In some cases, temporarily cooling the brain would be the right thing to do; it would cool 'the hot headed' - literally. But of much more importance for those in therapy, recovery depended on the agility and ability of the mind of the therapist to 'hold' the patients mind as it *expanded.* I became very concerned for the patient who finds themselves in the clinic with a 'closed minded' therapist. In a lecture I asked, "if the patient goes to the therapist for counselling and the therapist to their supervisor, who does the supervisor go to?" The question was met by a blank stare from my teacher, who finally mumbled, "another therapist." 'Oh great,' I thought, 'so we all just regurgitate each others' rubbish, as if in some horrible game of pass the rubbish parcel; and what happens if the therapist's mind is more closed than our own?' The answer wasn't good enough for me, but in that moment I heard one in the back of my mind that was. It answered loud and clear and said, "you come back to Me."

Artists, such as Michelangelo, of course knew very well what they were doing. They knew of and manipulated for our own good, a natural human tendency of curiosity; whenever a gap appears within artwork, or indeed anything, the curious would not be able to resist the temptation to peer in. Ambiguous gaps enabled an inquisitive observer the space within which to question, not only the artist's, but their own psychic truths. They were necessary spaces within which all perceivers might explore and perhaps find a missing, forgotten part of themselves. Gaps were the 'vital omissions' that turned a painting into a masterpiece; and a mind into a Universe.

The artists I studied were not eccentrics with minds precariously wide open, they were multi-lingual geniuses who had been given the wisdom of Heaven. I concluded there are no mad artists, just those marvellous beings that communicate in a language often too long foreign for our own mortal ears and eyes to fathom - and I suppose sometimes, for their own too. Artists, like geniuses, were not those who were 'losing it'; they were the ones who were getting 'it'. In sculptures and paintings of religious encounters, are often found solutions to the problems we are all facing today. Religion was never the problem or root of all evil, ignorance was, and *'The Moses'* carried something incredibly precious under his arm – knowledge. The face of the prophet reveals he is clearly wondering how to impart the knowledge of Heaven to the masses – the tribe who had investment in not knowing. Knowledge is the key to survival, not only physical, but psychological and spiritual as well. Whilst ignorance seeks only to keep us blind, distant, separate, fearful and bound; knowledge reveals to reform, console, amend and set us all free. Simply put, ignorance seeks always to terminate; knowledge seeks only to regenerate. Of all the things that one can ingest, it is knowledge that offers the optimum immunity.

> *"He who learns much, unlearns all violent desiring"*
>
> Friedrich Nietzsche *(1883-1885 – Thus Spoke Zarathustra)*

An old friend once commented that when she looked for the first time at *'The David'*, she cried. It was easy to see why. Whilst *'The Moses'* had seemed mysteriously ambiguous, *'The David'* by total contrast, was staggeringly honest. The name 'David' translates as 'Beloved' and the statue spoke not only of a physical story, of the moment a young boy overcame the giant Goliath, but spoke of an emotional, psychological story as well. Devoid of all apparent defences and the add-on regalia that make up a multiplicity of imagery, *'The David'* depicted the absolute essence of man in his purest form – and he was naked. Naked of the contaminants of this world and all its expectations. It is a statue that has brought tears to many an eye and I would suggest not only due to the recognition of a brilliant artist, but in remembrance of ones own 'naked' innocence. *'The David'* is a symbol of triumph over adversity, it was crafted not through the eyes of idolisation but adoration – just as we all are. *'The David'* refers us back to the strengths within our imagination, before it became projected into and confined within a fear based framework. We are more than just our bodies and *'The David'* reminds us that when faced with apparently overwhelming odds, it is within the innocent heart and the imaginative youthful mind, that we find our real strength of spirit; where children have always the power to humble giants - and lambs the protection of God.

My Poetry

Presented within my artwork, my poems, are the 'real life' experiences of people whose hearts and minds are in various stages of evolution. Some when despair came crashing through the boundaries, others when the light that follows flooded in. Whilst it would have been easy to produce a book that only contained poetry to uplift the spirit, that would have been just half of what is the human story. Happiness is generally not something we struggle or 'need' others help with - sadness often is. In some poems I have written of broken hearts, of minds in turmoil and confusion; in others I write of happiness, joy, companionship and the ultimate experience of an infusion of grace. My poetry follows a typical, archetypal, *a-typical* pathway of experience; with the poems set out sequentially, more or less in parallel with a chronological evolution of the ego, and rise in conscious comprehension, as follows:-

Part I.

In Part I, is presented the encounters of the inner and outer child. It is an exposition of the emotional experiences of the child that lives forever in the heart; and the many challenges it faces. The inner child is our first experience with this world, and I would suggest, is also our last. Most of the poetry in this section descended as I worked alongside children, who it seemed, had incarnated with agendas to suffer - early and a lot. They inevitably taught me well. Whilst I thought I had always been quick, they were often quicker, though perhaps only physically so. In their speed to rush through life, chuck out anything that didn't immediately satiate or threatened to burn out soon, I saw hurt children throwing 'their babies' out with the bathwater; just as they must have felt thrown out too. They took no prisoners because their cells were already full up! Confused, angry, alone and bound by wounds received, as many are, in childhood. But I also saw beyond the 'tough acts' into the glowing hearts of little children, asking as they do, for evidence that somebody could see who they were; that it was safe to be in this world and that someone, somewhere cared. I wrote them poetry to show that I did. In return, what can I say of when those children smiled? They simply had the power to light up the world.

Part II.

In part two, is referred 'my theory' of a fourth stage of ego; that seeks for reparation, reconciliation and repair, though often acts in spite of itself. It is beyond the superego and I call it 'the mature ego': referring to its maturation and old age, its grandfather status. It is not the inflated ego and less the ego trip or altered state, but more the contented ego and the flight or rocking state. As the ego evolves the outer eyes close and the inner eye opens - the spiritual one. As the third eye opens within the mind, it casts forth an array of psychological and spiritual experiences; that can cause more than a wobble to even the most enlightened mind. With the energy flowing through the heart, reconnecting with the mind, love, and in spiritual terms light, enters into the darkest recesses or caves of the unconscious. This is the time when dreams continue on into the waking hours; when their symbolic meaning is mysteriously reproduced in daily life. Whether we like it, or feel able to endure it or not, the wounds sitting in memories from this life, or any other for that matter, are projected out into our everyday realities. Within this section is described the phenomena that emerges in parallel with a mind in a high state of evolution: as the dying ego reluctantly sheds a skin, the rising phoenix symbolises the re-birth of our Selves. Psychologically, this can be a difficult time and certainly it is not easy to function as before, particularly if in apparent communication with spirits that others are not able to see – or certainly will never admit to. At this, the most vulnerable stage of 'ego evolution', when Jung's synchronicity ensures the frequency dial is turned up fully, more than Providence attempts to move in. But it is also a time of rest, regeneration, replenishment and renewal; a time when Heaven takes over, wiping the inherited belief patterns off the unconscious slate. Even though one can feel quite 'spaced out', they can be sure at least Heaven knows what it is doing; and it does so with the purest intention. Grace is always on our side. Certainly, it is better to have awareness of an empty or confused mind, than no awareness of a mind full-up with the fixated opinions of what other people think. At this time there emerges a good opportunity to ask oneself the question, 'what do I think?' It is shortly followed by others such as, 'who am I anyway?' The early stage of ego maturation is often a time of humiliating and humbling experiences; and plenty of tears. Though once we have cleared the debris of ego inflated images of who we are not, we open up a pathway to experience the truth of who we really are. Ego evolutions are often painful, but then, who would really want to stay in a cave of illusions when there is a sunny garden within which to play? - even if we have to walk through a forest; the garden is always still there.

Part III.

In part three is described the moment in which an explosion of bliss floods the system with the ecstatic experience of a Divine love requited. It is a celebration of the spectrum of love in all its colours; a time when we 'walk on air', or in spiritual language, when the spirit temporarily leaves the body and flies through the ether. When the *kundalini rises*, there are few words though sweet smells are aplenty. Should one have lost sight of their saviour, this is the time when Heaven 'sends a soul to save ya'. The heart overflows with a higher love like never before. It is the time, should we believe in a soul mate, that they enter into our lives, reflecting the true colours within our hearts. When love requites, all that is found in the material realm is transcended. It is a reminder of the purity and power of unconditional love; that gives us the strength to finally let go and move on.

Part IV.

In part four, is described a bizarrely amazing experience in which the truly magical shows up. The mystical phenomena that exceed all rational logic, appears in correlation with a 'quantum leap' in human consciousness; due to both existing at the same high frequency. Strange, oh yes very strange, but no less true! The mystical is absolutely phantastical. It is beyond earthly human comprehension, or even, discussion. The magic, or rather, the *Magi* enter and revelations are staggeringly aplenty. Humour rises in correlation with silence and prayer; as we see life from a comical big picture. Thank goodness, thank God-ness.

Part V.

When first designing the layout out this book, part five was at one time part six, though it is here that this particular compilation now ends; with a collection of prophetic poems that I trust will speak for themselves. The 'missing part', currently in feather, may appear in another volume, though it is perhaps for the strictly esoteric astronaut. I end this section with at least two 'curiosities' to think about: the first, that Pandora never opened the box in the first place; and secondly, that even Willy Wonka could not have offered a more golden ticket for the reader - who really does already have everything they need.

My poems, as the analyst might say, are descriptions of my *counter transference experiences.* Most were written for and about other people; some after I met with them in person; others, such as *'The boy behaving badly'*, was written about an adolescent that I never met.

Of all the poems that descended, whether written well or with a licence borrowed from anything other than a poet, there are some that I simply adore more than others. I love the 'dumbfounded-ness' in *'The wizard of us'*, that I wrote in a coffee shop at University; and the recognition of the sublime and the ridiculous in *'The comedy of life'*. And whilst *'The Venus returns'* is a fast contender for my heart, *'The best place I can be'* leaves a warmth that permeates my soul.

In poetry, painting and children's stories we therefore find not only descriptions of the human experience, but the spiritual one as well. Should any reader find that they leave Oz only to enter into Alice's wonderland, then you have both my admiration and compassion; though you might find comfort in remembering that there is always a lion where there is a witch and a wardrobe; and hares can be cuddly, if not a little late! Ultimately, the Tin Woodman lives forever within you. Life, after all, is the greatest story and we are all living in it today, together. No one needs to feel alone, as Lord Byron wonderfully said, "in solitude we are least alone". Love can enter in at any moment. In life, tomorrow is always another day in which things can get better and who knows, perhaps the best days are yet to come for all of us. Changes in life can leave us feeling vulnerable, it can get wobbly, bizarre and turbulent, but such is the rich tapestry. That which we consistently fail to appreciate, is that we are all authors of the stories in which we live; and since the pen is still in our hands, it is never too late to write in a happy ending.

We are all on a journey and it is the task of every soul to dig their way out of the shadows of ignorance and find the courage to fly into the sunshine. Life is full of pitfalls, trauma and tears and yet in every travesty there is always an opportunity for growth, and perhaps even the chance for humour. Mastering the art of merging ambiguities is a work of psychic art in itself, but where-else might opposing realities convene if not in the unconscious psyche and infinite imagination of man? It is an illogical experience and a mystical phenomenon, but another reminder nevertheless, that as the artist man is not only able to produce a timeless masterpiece in which he exists, but a collective reality in which all humankind exists; a reality, that is after all, Divinely created in the original mind of pure perfection and projected in multiple unison through the minds of us mortals; out onto the ultimate canvas - the primal screen we call life.

For you then, the traveller, may you remember in times of chaos that you are never closer to giving birth to the dancing stars of poets and painters, of sculptors and dreamers; and may you travel through your life knowing, that love is the eternal companion for your journeying soul.

Part I.

For the Inner and Outer Child

Loss

So quickly as I turned my head
I fell into despair
For when I turned it back again
I found you were not there

So silently you did depart
Before my eyes could see
In shock I feared you disappeared
And can not now save me

Now mourning loss and double cross
Perceive as it would seem
That all I had is gone and bad
I'm left to wish a dream

In truth I know as I should grow
That troubles come and pass
But cold I stand in sinking sand
And beg that I may ask

If life contains just your remains
Then I can't pay the cost
Please now to take my heart that break
For I can't bear your loss

Little Child

Little child your eyes reveal
A life behind that you conceal
Where happiness in memories are
Where brightness lights your dancing star

If only for this moment know
Whilst anxious don't you buy sorrow
Dig deep to find the strength within
Release you from a crimeless sin

Step bravely in tomorrow's sight
And laugh the shadows of the night
That secretly are friends of old
If only we withstood the cold

Imagination is your gift
As you believe your spirit lift
And bring you back to save a soul
Where you will find yourself as whole

Let go the monsters of the past
Sit still within your mind at last
And listen for the voice inside
That always will with you reside

Judge you not stupidity
But understand in life should be
Better things than cleverness
Like gentle gifts of pure kindness

A constant thing in life is change
When circumstances rearrange
But never lose sight of the fact
That change is not a skill you lack

Go forward and believe it's true
The life you want is up to you
And know no matter what appear
That love is always found in fear

…to an Abuser

Too young to truly know my fate
Too young to run and hide
Too young to know in years to come
That you stole then my pride

How could you ever violate
How could you never cry
How don't you know you left behind
A child wishing to die

How cruel to burn your mark on me
How cruel to denigrate
How dare you steal my trust away
And cause my heart to break

But most of all I can't believe
Just how it came to be
That as you took my innocence
You gave your hate to me

Miss Perception

You see trouble and disaster
You see thunderstorms and rain
I see happy ever after
I see peace beyond the pain

You feel bitter and resentful
You feel helpless and remote
I feel humble truly grateful
I feel I may keep afloat

You stay waiting in the distance
You believe that fear is real
I am running to the future
I believe the love I feel

You think you cannot recover
You think it's alright for me
I think you don't know my cover
Know not of my history

You see ugliness and loathing
You see scars upon your heart
I see loveliness in clothing
I see beauty that thou art

You see victim in the mirror
But one day you will perceive
That I am just your reflection
And you will be truly free

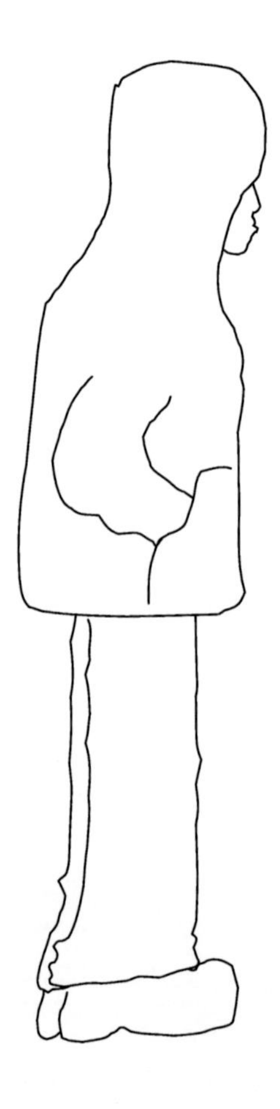

The Boy Behaving Badly

To you the boy who shouts within
Behaving badly, driving sin
What you don't know
What they can't see
Is just how brave you are to me

I see a child, I see a man
Standing lonely, craving hands
To hold you as you learn and grow
And take away pain of sorrow

But child look deeply at your soul
You are not broke, you are one whole
And you must find the flame inside
That flickers in your wounded pride

For you are handsome, bright and strong
And you must celebrate your song
And see that in your darkest hour
That deep inside you have the power

So hand me back all of your tears
And look forward to all the years
When you will learn to love and be
The man who in the boy I see

My Darling Dear

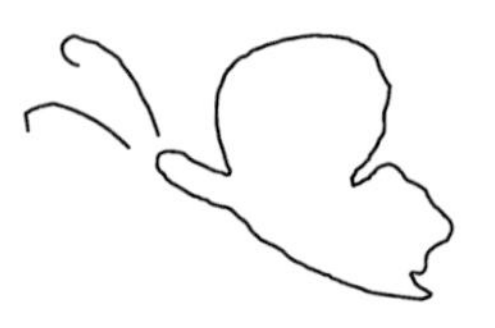

You never knew that I could see
The angel in your heart
You never thought that I might know
Just what beauty thou art

You never could see through my mind
To know who I might be
But always did I look at you
To fall upon my knee

You are the summer in my life
The rainbow in my soul
You are the baby in my arms
The breath that makes me whole

You are the wonder of the world
The girl who leads the rest
You are the fire within my veins
The shield upon my chest

You are the air that guides my flight
My whisper on the wind
You are the sparkling in the night
When no-one else will mend

You are the beacon on the shore
Amazing as you shine
You are my drops of honey dew
My drink of summer wine

You are all that I never was
You are all I wished for
Your kisses are beyond compare
You are all I adore

You are the strength I wish I knew
Seduced within your grasp
A true creation of a life
My love will ever last

No matter what you think within
What ever does appear
You are the jewel within my heart
You are my darling dear

To a Carer from a Child

I HIT YOU because I have been hit

I SPIT at you because I am so full up with other peoples' spite

I *scratch* your arms because I do not know how to ask you for a hug

I kick your legs because I cannot stand on mine

I frighten you because I am really so afraid of you

I reject you because I have been rejected

I bite you because my soul has been bitten

I punch your face because I cannot bear you to look at how ugly I feel

I hurt you because I have only learned how to hurt

And I hate you because

I do not know

how to love you..

... but I ask for your forgiveness, for I am only a child;

Please see past my behaviour to see me

Have faith that I am still in there on the inside

and accept me

Walk into my mind and greet me

Fly into my heart and free me

For this is how you will save me

This is how I will learn how to love me

Only then will I trust how to be me

Only then will you know that I thank you

Only then

will you know

that I love you.

Mommy

Come over here you little dear
Let mommy wipe your face
Did you fall down and break your crown
Do you feel in disgrace

Come to my smile and be a while
Let mommy ease your pain
My little soldier getting older
You do not fight in vain

Come to my breast and take a rest
For you are trying hard
And don't you fear I'll wipe your tear
Let mommy be your guard

Come to my womb the sacred tomb
From where your life began
And still the time when you are mine
Let mommy hold your hand

Come to my sight where you just might
Forgive you as I do
And see behind your troubled mind
To better parts of you

Come to my heart where you can start
To realise your worth
To me you are the brightest star
My Heaven here on Earth

Come to my side I'll be your guide
Adore you as you grow
My shining pin my little king
Your mommy loves you so

The Outer Child

I wonder what you will reveal
As you sit opposite me
I wonder what your heart will spill
As memories may you flee

I wonder what you will not say
As you distract my thought
I wonder what you will display
As souls are sold and bought

I wonder what you will not give
As I offer my mind
I wonder what you can not see
As visions are you blind

I wonder if you'll ever know
As you sit cold and wild
That you are not the only one
As I am too a child

Thinking of You

Oh child that thinks you're all alone
Lost the path that leads you home
And thus believe no other will
To call you from the window sill

But dear know you are not outside
But always will in hearts reside
Warm up your hands upon the fire
And let go your ego desire

This life is not as you might think
As hardly dry the pen and ink
When order shift and re-arrange
And though you fix the fix must change

Simple is in silence be
My tiny lamb of symphony
Let worries leave and lies depart
To re-instil your bless'ed heart

Nothing to fear no tears to cry
No more to quest to reason why
When all you have is all you need
As wound to heal must first to bleed

Breathe in the life that you were given
A gift for you from Love in Heaven
Unique your form a rainbow through
A child of God sweet child are you

Let Me

Let me wipe your tiny tears
Take away your silent fears
Lead you back through all the years
Guide you home to angel spheres

Cleanse your mind renew your soul
Know you faith and make you whole
Take the blame and pay your toll
Show you love for your console

Let me give though you should take
Hold your heart when it should break
Stand the ground though you may quake
Resolve the anger you create

Let me heal the hurt inside
Withstand the pain that you abide
As I can see though you should hide
And I can be where you reside

Let me mend your broken wing
Renew your song and hear you sing
Light the way when it gets dim
Amend the game so you can win

Let me guide if you should fall
I'll be behind if you should call
I'll hold your hand and stand you tall
I'm here beside and through it all

Let you be what you forgot
Impossibilities are not
Release your mind untie the knot
Remember all that you begot

Let not you grieve your troubled past
Let not you fear tomorrows fast
Take now for you all in your grasp
And know that love can never pass

Part II.

Ego Evolution

I Wonder Who Mr Freud

I look at you and wonder who
I was ever meant to be
A part of you a part of who
a part of maybe me

Did you dictate did I create
in ways you wanted to
Did you achieve all I believe
and save a soul or two

Did we conspire did I desire
in thoughts we maybe danced
Were you the one my father son
did we a brief romance

When all it took was word and book
to write down our insight
We're past amend can't comprehend
the fleeing after fight

And yet I pray and bless the day
that we did happen past
And here I stand with cap in hand
and offer you my last

You took the line you made it shine
did all that you could do
In awe I stand in your command
and still I wonder who

The Wizard of Us

Life would be so much easier
If I didn't have to be
At each and every moment
Another version of me

If I only had the skills within
That I could draw upon

I wouldn't feel I'm losing out
On all I could become

They tell me that it's all in me
And I should look and find

But how can I see anything
When I'm completely blind

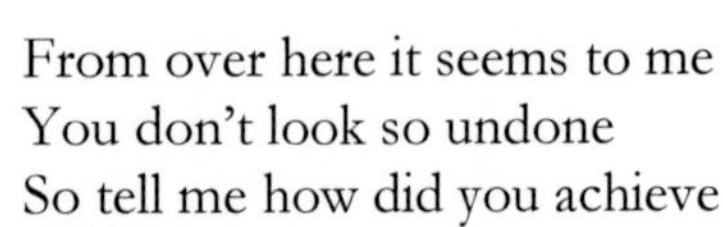

From over here it seems to me
You don't look so undone
So tell me how did you achieve
A million into one

For if I had your magic wand
To grant a wish or two
I'd wave it like a conductor
And change from me to you

I'd grant I had your confidence
I'd grant I had your heart
I'd grant I had the brains to know
That I won't fall apart

But most of all I'd wish for eyes
To help finally see
The pathway that will lead me to
The wonderful wizard of me

Fragmented Sanity

Where is this world that I exist
When I'm not drugged I'm down and pissed
I'm kicked and torn and in the mist
When I'm so low it's hard to miss

Why do you have to be so kind
Can you not see the ties that bind
What consequence my shattered mind
Suspends me fearful leaves me blind

What is this life this rotten hole
Where is my heart where is my soul
Where is the care won't you console
Why do I have to bear it all

What is the point of all the pain
When I can't see beyond the rain
When all is lost it's all in vain
When all I think is I'm insane

Tell me something I don't know
Tell me how to bear sorrow
Tell me why and tell me now
Tell me I'll live and show me how

Alpha Encore

So you think no-one can comprehend just where your mind might go
Imagine you are all alone and no-one else could know
The first to find the last to leave and lost somewhere between
No feet on earth in your rebirth and nothing as it seem

See shadows dancing in your dream dodge stalkers of the night
Submerged in fastest flowing stream fall from the greatest height
No-one to hear your silent fear no hand to grasp and hold
No courage left within your heart that once was young and bold

But here's the truth said loud and clear that surely you must sense
That this is not a time begot but space for recompense
No ghastly sight can you perceive without first you create
No demon stand crossed hallowed land where angel at the gate

My dear you see all you could be both fact and mystic fiction
Extract from this eternal bliss enabled in your diction
Can you now tell that this no spell but gift from Ether given
Revealed today so you might say I found my soul in Heaven

No matter what the path you trod to bring you to this state
Important now is when and how and know it's not too late
For blessed you are a golden star is handed from behind
In time will eyes clear misty skies that once where closed and blind

How happy might your life become if only you believed
That all was found when left the ground and once more you perceived
Unfolding wings tucked in your jeans new warrior of one
Your life not end when you descend but once more has begun

Killing Me Softly

You can not go
You can not leave
For without you
I can not breathe

I can not see
Without your eyes
All that's in me
I do despise

What do you mean
You won't be here
I have no hope
You've no idea

If you won't heal
My bleeding heart
Without your love
My life depart

And of tomorrow
I can't think
Because today
My spirit sink

You must not love
Without my kiss
You must not breathe
Without my lips

I have no choice
No reality
For without you
I have not me

Petrified
Isolated fear
My terror island
Has no pier

A life in hell
And all I know
You must not leave
You can not go

In Honour of The Death of the Ego

I feel lonely, isolated
And it's not much fun in here
I feel distant, disconnected
Have a mind that's full of fear

I feel sad within my sorrow
And I really can't conceive
It will all be fine tomorrow
In a new way I'll perceive

I feel angry, disappointed
That it all happened to me
And I really cannot thank you
Though you wait on bended knee

I feel bitter in my language
Feel the victim that I am
Know that when my life is over
I will go where souls are damned

I feel shut-out and abandoned
Wonder what's the point of life
If I struggle in the darkness
To become a sacrifice

I feel lost within my being
And I'm losing touch with me
As I watch my world fragmenting
Meet my own insanity

I feel terror as I'm dying
Cannot catch the breath I need
I hear angels softly crying
As my heart begins to bleed

I feel cold within the silence
As I wait for God to take
All the souls afraid of dying
Hardly in my bones I quake

I feel still within my absence
As I watch the morning dawn
And I pray the worst is over
Save my passing left to mourn

But I've peace within the stillness
And I wonder what will be
As I feel my God descending
Standing there at back of me

I feel new within my rebirth
As I finally begin
Handing back all of my sadness
Handing back my only sin

That I never could conceive it
That I ever could believe
That I would live past my dying
That I could be truly free

Male Avail

Try to move but I'm not sure
Demons knocking at my door
Want to find my better side
Not sure where it might reside

Terrified to look behind
Scared I know just half my mind
Wonder what might lie within
What trouble caused what fallen sin

Feel uneasy in my step
Trying hard but still not yet
One more turn one twist of fate
Release me from the Devil's gate

But what is this I think I see
No demon stands in front of me
As time unfold illusion part
I see an Angel in my heart

Can it be true I have no shame
Only my soul for me to claim
In hope I stand before thy shrine
To take back now what once was mine

Thank you my gift in mystery
Helped me to clear the mist for me
Hardly believe it can be true
I found that part of me in you

Truly blessed in my redeem
Heaven sing within my dream
Believe in faith that now I see
Remember love as it should be

Not A Hero

Will you love me, if I'm not a hero
Will you hold me if I fall
Will you ignore my inhibitions
Will you accept me warts and all

If I said I'm not a warrior
Could not save you from a fire
Would you know that I still love you
Still adore you and desire

Should it be I have no white horse
No sword, no gallant heart
Would you forgive another dreamer
Who has loved you from the start

And if I said I'd never leave you
Give you all I had to give
Might you see that in my weakness
I have still the strength to live

So will you take the aging hand dear
Of a boy, sometimes a beast
Who has just a broken heart here
But I would give you that, at least

Double Crossed

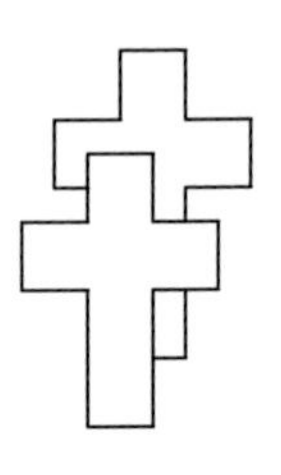

Smooth-talkers and abusers let the story now be told
Conmen and confusers in a life so tired and old
See through your disguises to the souls that you have sold
Know from your surprises seek a heart that's made of gold

Pass along your parcels full of all the tales of woe
Pitiful the rascals who would ever steep so low
Think you can't be trusted with the time that you now throw
Truly am disgusted by the lengths that you would go

What use have I of tricksters who would seek my chastity
Steal my love in bruises take all that belongs to me
Jealous of my freedom envy all that I can see
What good is a seducer with a lost identity

In treacherous deceivers find a daemon lost and mad
In wounded disbelievers smell the ghost of hurt and sad
But sent are you to teach me how to value all I have
And trust my intuition to discern the good from bad

So keep you all a distance who have come to seek my love
In half your mind that sleeping know you're watched from up above
And know not in a million would I take a fallen glove
From any one chameleon who has not the wings of dove

Beyond the Mask

When I can see beyond the veil
Into your gifted soul
Why do you have to drag me down
Into the darkest hole

When I can know your brightest light
Why can you still not see
That far beyond the image shines
The brightest light in me

When all I find within your heart
Is innocent perfection
Why do you break the very glass
Revealing your reflection

When I have been through hell and back
To save you from your fate
Why do you fear when I return
And tell me I'm too late

When all I see within your mind
Is honesty so pure
Can you not see that all I do
Is offer you a cure

When I will fight on your behalf
Remind you of above
Can it be right that you deny
My simple gift of love

When I can see the God in you
Why does it have to be
That you seem so afraid of truth
To see the God in me

From Egos to Eros

~ for those afraid to dance

What then?

If you can not perceive
Then you do not believe
If you can't understand
You dismiss out of hand

If you can not the fear
Then you wield up the spear
Then you can not desire
And you can not aspire

But shame is the most
If you can not the ghost
And life is but lost
If you will not the cost

If you could only see
Then you could see through me
Not from Ego as seems
For it all through the dreams

That insanity by-pass
As it's all but a farce
To obscure what is true
What is there in all you

No neurosis in sight
But a soul in mid flight
So not wise to concern
For the fun will you earn

To believe all you need
To know truth to proceed
That it was all along
In the words of life's song

That the heart can then rest
And you'll never detest
With the beauty in soul
Fuse you back to one whole

Lead you not to your end
But from where you descend
Through the eyes of adore
To His love ever more

Part III.

Requited Love

The Beautiful Rose

Enigmatic in its beauty
Though the bud has yet to bloom
Stills the moment in a lifetime
Steals the twine from off the loom

Softly frozen in potential
Whilst it looses not a gasp
So appealing in its splendour
Sits the rose within the vase

True antiquity in motion
Though the story yet untold
Delicately most revealing
As the petals now unfold

To display a deeper meaning
To romance the bravest heart
Whispers poetry whilst breathing
Lest the melody depart

Reflecting innocent devotion
Of a love so pure and true
Reminds the heart beyond the potion
Of the beauty that's in you

May you always then remember
Whilst the years may come to pass
That my love will be forever
Though the rose evade the glass

And no matter where I wander
And no matter where life goes
Ever last for you in Heaven
Is my love beside the rose

The Best Place I Can Be

The best place I can be
Is in my phantasy
Where all is bold
And knights of old
Ride past in majesty

For here I spread my wings
Where all the heaven sings
The pipes rejoice
I've found my voice
Surrounded by my kings

Where all the spirits fly
And with them so do I
And in my heart
My soul can start
To bring you to the sky

Though in this life I know
The rope that we must tow
I still must weave
As I perceive
So in their hearts they glow

For in this baron land
Their castles built on sand
If I don't pass
Across the vast
And take them in my hand

But you and I are one
In colours of the sun
Where God above
Can see our love
And where our shadows run

And all has turned to gold
Though life we may grow old
But I now see
For you and me
Our thoughts in manifold

Though humble in my bone
Must love the undertone
And bless the day
They came my way
And led me to the throne

And now forever more
I've opened up the door
To life anew
For me and you
Where love is all I saw

A place where there's no fear
Where healing in the tear
Where miracles
Like icicles
Come down from there to here

And as I take your hand
We dance in other land
And in reverse
Through poem and verse
I'll guide you to the man

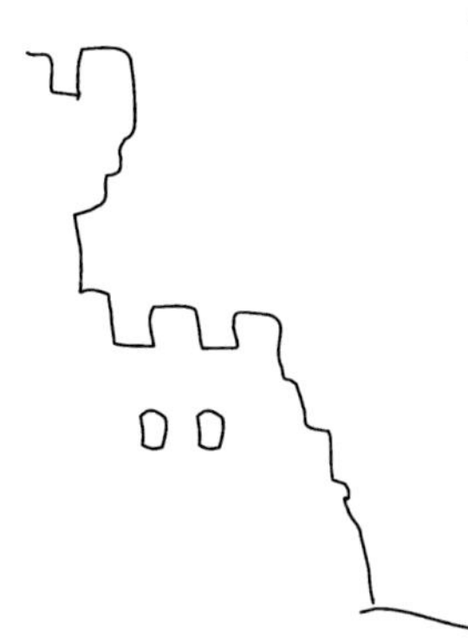

Where never can despair
Where you will find me there
Where love can bring
All everything
To our castle in the air

After All…

In your presence I felt thunder and rain
I thought images that drove me insane
In your company I threatened to leave
In the silence I started to grieve

In your gaze I felt ugly and lost
Knew I could never pay what you cost
Saw the look in your tiring eyes
Had the sense it was me you despise

But it once wasn't always this way
Thinking back to a late summer day
When the leaves turned from copper to gold
And my life was not lonely and cold

Was a thrill to know you were alive
In this dream where we dance to survive
Found an angel with tender warm kisses
With a pocket of love and good wishes

Know that life should evolve and go on
Hear the sound of an old distant song
Close my eyes to remember your face
Try a humbling prayer full of grace

In your presence I felt childish and small
Thought I could always handle it all
In your company fell a tear one or two
But in your absence I know I love you

When You Smiled

You smiled…	I breathed
You fed	I ate
You walked	I ran
You gave	I took
You stood	I stumbled
You held	I fell
You whispered	I shouted
You loved	I hated
You watched	I faltered
You saw	I found
You saved	I surrendered
You graced	I humbled
You led	I followed
You taught	I listened
You thought	I accepted
You shone	I believed
When you smiled	I remembered
That you are	… and I am

Affairs of the Heart

Humble me for I did cause the noisiest a din
Strayed from the path of righteousness into a mortal sin
Do not know from where it came or whence it happened last
Got swept away in psychic sway into a lovers grasp

Saw cherubs smiling in the eyes of sirens on the shores
But wonder just if in the lust saw paradise in whores
Heard Heaven call above it all knew lessons in the test
But were was hope upon to float when charmed by sweet temptress

Walked into flames of my remains to find the God inside
Though when return my heart still burn as if no God reside
Destined to dwell in caves of hell found paintings of the sky
Lost clarity within my mind lost meaning in the why

But what was this in twilight mist I glimpse in introspect
An opportunity for me in silent soul reflect
Was she a wolf in sheep's attire, was I a sacrifice
Or was she too the Angel who appeared in a disguise

At once I saw no rotten whore but innocence so pure
Remind me of forgotten parts of me that God adore
Felt phoenix rise in golden skies ascended through my heart
Know spirit came so I should gain a lost ancestral chart

Simple illusions in the mind that cause bodies to lust
When truth be told from men of old tis still question of trust
Emotion swirl in every girl reveals the lack in me
Purge my belief in hidden grief I fear intimacy

No serpent tempt but represent a love I'd misperceived
Important not when lesson got to beat a soul to bleed
Heard angels sing within the din received a bless'ed gift
Merge ambiguity on Earth to heal Etheric rift

Was no seduction of my soul no innocence I lost
Just sleepy dreams through which it seems destined to pay a cost
For in reality I gained the greatest of a chance
In brief affair where children dare found me within the dance

Goodbye

And now it's time to say goodbye
May break a heart or two
Hear someone in the Ether cry
When say goodbye to you

Though trembling fear put down the spear
Detach from kindest soul
To journey on where we belong
In faith return as whole

Shattered by the stones that flew
But always could I see
There behind the depths of you
Were deeper shades of me

Your Angel face reveal your grace
Pray you will meet the Self
That still exist through ego mist
In darkness find your wealth

When mirror crack reveal the lack
Think somehow past abuse
Trust on the Earth we find our worth
Know all shall know a use

So thank you for reflecting back
The parts I could not see
In image shine your pure Divine
Reflecting parts of me

Blessed to fly in Summer sky
With you beside my wing
Contract now end on self depend
In silence Heaven sing

Left just to say though stumble may
In truth we never part
Though lesson end forever friend
Give you my loving heart

In Memory of a Friend

In death where we have no power
No permission nor stance nor retort
In death where we have no language
No words no strength no thought

When a life too suddenly taken
And a friend so terribly lost
Leaves behind in a mind truly shaken
And a heart to aburden a cost

In a place between worlds rarely spoken
Lives a love in eternity bright
And a soul now immortally woken
And a candle to burn in the night

Precious memories to cherish forever
Silent moments of grace always given
And a friend once beside us to tether
Be they ever more peaceful in Heaven

Transcending Adam

Re-entered

Reminded

Reviewed

Re-worked

Restored

Replaced

Rejuvenated

Re-lived

Replenished

Reunited

Returned

Reconnected

Remembered

...Requited x

Part IV.

Mystical Phantastical

Pandora's Box

What path you walk to go and seek
What do you hope to find
What secret will you try to keep
What drive your searching mind

What destined role will you perform
What story will unfold
What phantasy will you transform
What hero to behold

What vision will you pray to see
What void you wish to fill
What sacrifice your quest to thee
What heart you hope to still

What Saviour call you from the dream
What Master shall you grace
What image change from all it seem
What silence may you face

What child you fight to try protect
What wings you hope to mend
What memory fade your soul perfect
What gift angelic friend

What mirror shall reflect within
What key to turn your locks
What light to caste mere mortal sin
From your Pandora's Box

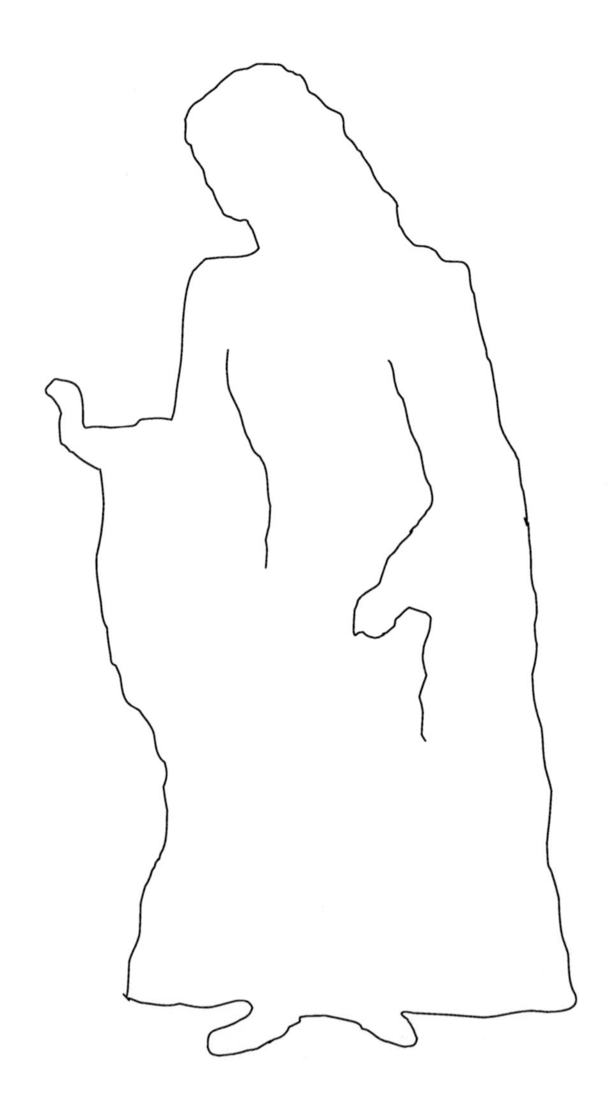

She

What is this in front of me
Dancing across the boundary
Happily within her grasp
Heaven in her mind at last

Look into her eyes and see
Parallel reality
Knows the truth that you do seek
Wake you dreamer from the sleep

Beauty flirting with the beast
Sacrifice dispel the feast
Purity in motion be
Innocent Divinity

Fear may rise but it will fall
She appear when Author call
Serenity upon her face
Humility in silent grace

Close the eye to walk the path
Of your illusion she will laugh
Trust in a heart where freedom fly
Angel ascend through mystic sky

Brave your heart and free your soul
Let go a half to know a whole
Hold the pretty hand of old
That bought the soul that once you sold

Delicate the trembling lamb
Ask of her just who I am
Elegance in poetry
A silhouette of Heaven - She

Dungeons and Drag Ons

All alone within your cell
Lost inside a private hell
See the bars that hold you in
Coldest iron of blackest tin

Cobbles wet as dampness rise
Illusion form through teary eyes
Breathing air from years before
No point in searching for the door

Gatekeeper come occasionally
To keep you blind so you can't see
Within your mind the power you need
Redeem your Self from others greed

Might it be so you misperceived
And though your innocence you grieve
The truth is that he came but lost
Whilst you retained he paid the cost

What of the courage still inside
What of the hope and joy you hide
Why sit when you possess the key
Imagination set you free

Upon your back a pair of wings
And as you stand so Heaven sings
Removing dungeons in your way
Bring you into the light of day

Old phantasies shall not contain
A soul so bright with life to gain
A future full of happiness
Where wounds will heal and hearts will bless

Might you then let go yesterday
Hold out your hand the Angel say
The choice is yours and all I do
Is show you of the love in you

Worth Weighting

Are in Heaven the scales that on one side she fails
        To appreciate the distance to date
In her one tiny soul pure of torment and whole
        Worth the millions that equal her weight

In a world full of blind cannot fathom her kind
        Always envy and spit on her fire
Though in truth they do beg pay with arm and a leg
        Should they fortune a longing desire

Only God in her mind knows the innocent kind
        Born of courage and bravest of heart
And a daemon who stalks in her path as she walks
        To prevent her from hell she depart

        Staring into abyss of temptation and mist
                Only faith her caduceus staff
        As she stumble and call watch the tears as they fall
                Are the Holy and one who would laugh …

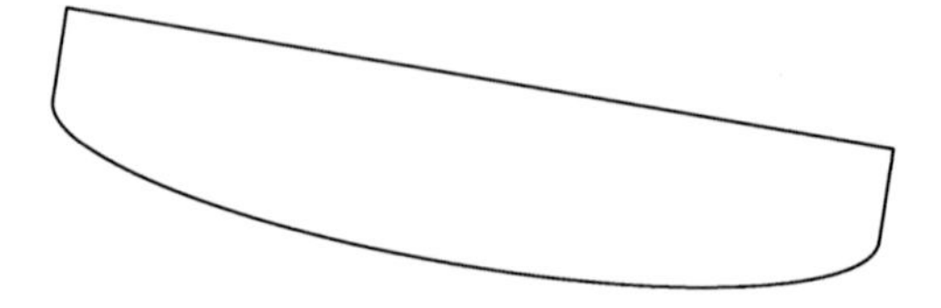

Now with trembling knees gave up all that would please
With a vision and willing to fly
Looks not down at the ground where the wretched resound
But attunes to a voice in the sky

Given more than all gold never empty nor cold
Sits the innocent lamb on the dish
And the battle begin between Heaven and sin
And illusion infuses her wish

To ascend even higher gave up all she desire
And awoke to the trickster inside
Saw the journey he took for the sceptre and hook
Ever wanting insatiable pride

With a quivering hand tiny soul took a stand
And refused to believe all he told
Found a voice locked away in new light of the day
Paid the piper now humble and old

Sit above all this land in the hand of a man
Who is everything greater than this
And in Heaven the scale tip for all she prevail
Loving God in her solitary bliss

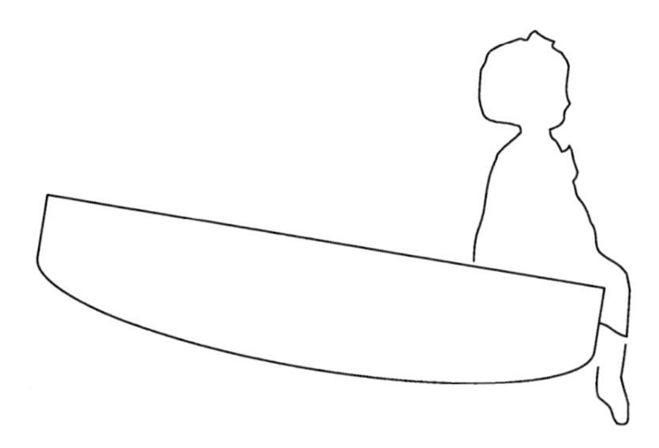

Ode to a Toad

I saw a man upon a road
Seemed burdened by his heavy load
But when enquired to his abode
I saw instead no man but toad

Realised the joke in this
Nay opportunity to miss
And so I begged the toad a kiss
Announced myself the toad mistress

Beamed a smile to slimy friend
And stole the kiss to my amend
In humour bowed my back to bend
Found truth in conscious comprehend

Was he a prince I hear you ask?
Was kissing him your golden task?
Did he transform unfold the past?
Did you upon your love at last?

Why mister happens you enquire
Perhaps a mistress you desire
Save you to quest for my inspire
Put down your load before you tire

The Sweet Release

Come closer and I'll show you this
A soul exist in love and bliss
And know no torture you create
No fear, no tear, no pain, no hate

Just simple stillness in the light
Released from shadows of the night
Exudes a glow of loveliness
Forgives all those forgot to bless

If life to teach then test to learn
To satiate a hunger burn
Evolving consciousness elate
Ascending grace through Heaven's gate

An easier path in death it seem
Lets go a dreamer from this dream
But truth be known so shall be told
Tis dream a myth of long and old

A moment might I wake you now
Remember when and where and how
Recall your soul from memories past
Requite a love that ever last

In kindness may I hold your hand
And trust in faith you'll understand
Can be no greater sweet release
Than finding beauty in the beast

The Angel

Behold that in thy darkest night
The Angel that is in thy sight
Brings forth the colours of true love
Transcend you to the Lord above

And whence thou heart begin to break
The deepest fear shall you create
In temporary sight you see
Where Angel now a beast shall be

But holdeth you to what is true
The innocence inside of you
Shall sweep the darkness clear away
Illuminating all in day

And you shall know what Angel bring
The truth so that your heart can sing
Releasing you into the dark
Blessed your journey did embark

So fear you not for it's not true
The truth is there inside of you
Not shadow but the purest light
To guide thee through the darkest night

So grace thou bravest Angel bring
You back to God and back again
That you shall live as you should be
Perfection lives inside of thee

For innocence and love is true
The Angel see inside of you
Your simple beauty you shall know
Return to life so you can grow

Humble child you shall not mourn
The darkest night before thy dawn
Shall come to pass and be thy gift
The freedom of thy spirit lift

The Angel that bring you to sleep
Doth wake you still, your soul you keep
And bless the path that you will see
The God that is inside of thee

May I ......?

May I call on the Elders
To show me the way
May I sing to the Spirits
To come down and play

May I whisper sweet nothings
To all who pass by
May I shine in the darkness
To light up the sky

May I breathe in the stillness
To fill up my soul
May I dance in the star-shine
To make me feel whole

May I sleep on a moonbeam
To soften my rest
May I speak of tomorrow
To be thankful and blessed

May I wish in this lifetime
To be all that I can
May I fly in the sunshine
To befriend who I am

May I turn to my maker
To gaze at his face
May I dream of a future
To know of my place

May I stop in the moment
To remember a kiss
May I always see rainbows
May I ask all of this

Illusion Opticus

Freeze the frame so you might see
Beyond the veil to deep in me
Release the catch that holds me here
And still the time for eyes to clear

Exposure dawn through mist and hue
Enigma be in front of you
Revealing of the inner calm
In silent pose in mid transform

Strange beauty stranger beast reside
Convert the wish revert the tide
Suspend the helix in your mind
Should misperceive clarity blind

A multitude of fabric make
The image now that you create
So woven in through all the years
So steeped within the love and tears

Capture naked deep reflection
Holographic pure perfection
Graceful flight on solid ground
From shattered glass to crystal sound

Photographs in black and white
Tranquillity in day and night
Collage my soul but do you see
The mystery inside of me

Part V.

The Prophecies

The Venus Returns

Tread softly lest you waken her
For you shall not beguile
Nor learn that taught or fathom thought
From Mona Lisa smile

Oh gentlemen of princely pen
Best not the lily gild
If half a mind then half be blind
Forever to bewilde

In grace ne'er lust or turn to dust
And never may you quest
Nor steal a kiss nor share a wish
Nor sleep upon her breast

Oh mother's son may you be one
The moment you concede
Within her power could she devour
Or set a tiny seed

Tis men of old that happen gold
Whenever he confess
A mystery from Heaven she
Both Angel and temptress

Take second chance and second glance
A faint heart never earn
And know her will when time stand still
The Venus shall return

Dear Physicist

So dearest is the physicist
Upon a quest he will persist
And one day find that what he sought
Was joy of life and peace of thought

In Petri dish a holy grail
When frequency will light a veil
As oscillations from the past
Reveal to him a truth at last

Still seeks in vitro to explain
Plasticity within the brain
And only in the physical
To understand umbilical

In cellular reality
Forgot a missing part of thee
Exploring answers in the dish
In parallel a mind does wish

Does life make sense from microscope
In secret keep his soul in hope
That courage still exist in form
To guide him past familiar norm

Organic view might you not see
That life above polarity
From bottom up you seek a clue
From Heaven down see all of you

From mother's cord to apron strings
And Nature's hoard to angels wings
Be astrocyte in front of you
With astral sight to guide you through

Dear physicist should stop in time
Reality no more is thyne
When silent words beg telepathic
Shall comprehend in holographic

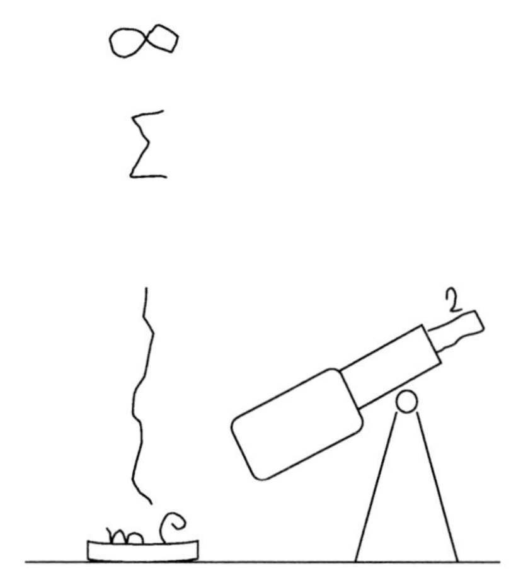

Silent Time

Know it be true

That He be thyne

Release in you

A blessed rhyme

To life anew

In pure refine

To see you through

The silent time

The Prophecy

And so the mind circles the sun
That He shall soon return as one
And His resolve is now His task
To re-arrange the troubled past

Cast demon from the blackest hole
Shall not consume tormented soul
But elevate and set thy sight
Above the terrors of the night

When Angels in the Heaven sing
Dispel the Devil from the wing
To glow amongst the hearts of man
Ascend him from thy troubled sand

In spirit of the greatest plan
Grace shadows of the troubled man
Surrender Him into thy glow
And all thy secrets you will know

The plight of man lay in your grasp
Can you believe tomorrow's gasp
Will be your choice and no one else
Can save them from thy troubled selves

Keep mystery which you can see
Deep heart of generosity
They know no mind compared to thee
Misunderstand not one but three

And seven kings will know thy fate
As seven counsels will create
And silence fall from Universe
To silence minds from troubled curse

Con't .....

Dissolve thy fear that not exist
Tread ancient stair and part thy mist
Know innocence within the lamb
Now purity within thy hand

As Anima whispers the truth
So ego rise and fold thy use
When serpent no more will project
Unconscious sleep of thy reject

Dream on thy dreams and you will know
Harmonize and you will grow
From Alpha through Omega bring
Enlightened bell of change now ring

When season turn from four to one
When man shall be His Fathers son
When water rise and water fall
When horsemen come to prophet's call

And time will cease though it not start
And man will break his troubled heart
When 100 monkeys tilt thy brink
The Earth shall move and land shall sink

Take twenty from twice middle age
When salt turns gold as muttered sage
Still feathered pens the story told
In painted caves from days of old

Look back to see infinity
Leap tempts to dwell insanity
Trick trickster from thy loving breast
Faith in belief to thyne attest

External space there shall not be
Across dimensionality
Through frequency to thy rotate
As satellites associate

Sweet Angels hear a trumpets song
As Heaven calls where we belong
In vortex swirls of souls depart
And we return where once we start

In mirror of Divinity
Shall see thy self and thy shall be
In perfect synchronicity
In gardens of pure ecstasy

The Comedy of Life

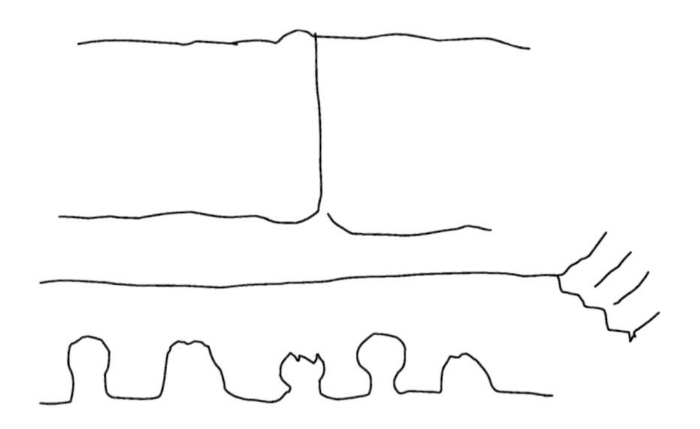

Then suddenly the image flipped
And changed from dark to light
I saw that in reflection was
A path to my delight

Upon the stage found actors who
Were beautiful in form
That in their majesty could caste
Mere phantasy transform

I laughed inside for I could tell
That this was no mistake
My misperception of pure hell
Redeemed in double take

But though the trickster raised a hand
To strike me from the stage
I laughed at him to overcome
That he should have no rage

And as the clown in true disguise
Reduced to tiny space
I know I saw in briefest time
A smile upon his face

For he was no more foolish than
The person I'd become
And as he held a hand to me
We alchemised as one

No gender based identity
Can take from man so wise
In truest form of dignity
Saw God within his eyes

Can you believe that this should be
A play in which we act
To take it no more seriously
Than matter of a fact

Amazing intellect to make
A tapestry of life
That held no more reality
Than illusions born in strife

When feeling stopped but eyes perceived
I found in front of me
No tragic consequence of fate
But Divine'st comedy

In Dreams We Seek

When trees uproot
And Nature screams
To falling planes
In mystic dreams
And shadows loom
And fires burn
When fishbones fall
Shall wings return
Greenest eyes
To quench a thirst
For angels food
And souls rebirth
In swimming pools
On winding stairs
Glimpse miracles
And timeless airs
Phallusies to prophecies
On axis to sublimity
Afraid to grieve
Too weak to dance
Then Pegasus
Turn brilliance
Shall Babylon elucidate
To bowing trolls illuminate
From stolen cars
To rivers deep
In bluest groves
Where dragons sleep
On mountain tops
Shall eagle land
And dove transform
On hallowed ground
When mirrors shine
Known lovers meet
Where pure Divine
In dreams we seek

The Angelical Stone

To pursue the celestial being
When elements balanced abound
And a heart be the weight of a feather
And the grace be too beautifully found
Rarely seen in a world often blinded
Be an angel that ne'er more hidden
When in darkness the Isis be lighted
And the fallen forever forgiven
Dream the alchemist findeth a reason
Where no reason can offer a plan
And philosophers turn into season
When a child stand in truth of a man
Sense the touch of a feminine whisper
Shine through eyes of a magical stone
Then a son be more closer to ether
And a soul that more onward to home

A Gift

From one to three
A journey far
I give to thee
A morning star
In love you be
Assured you are
From Maccabee
To Merkabah

... and as the lock turned,

Pandora opened the box.

Not out of disobedience, curiosity,

naivety or ignorance,

but in faith, fortitude,

wisdom and love.